T0129760

The
UNCOMMON WOMAN
of
FAITH
in the
MARKETPLACE

DR. BRANDY F. GIBSON

authorHOUSE®

AuthorHouse™
1663 Liberty Drive
Bloomington, IN 47403
www.authorhouse.com
Phone: 1 (800) 839-8640

© 2019 Dr. Brandy F. Gibson. All rights reserved.

No part of this book may be reproduced, stored in a retrieval system, or transmitted by any means without the written permission of the author.

Published by AuthorHouse 05/21/2020

ISBN: 978-1-7283-3758-6 (sc)
ISBN: 978-1-7283-3757-9 (e)

Library of Congress Control Number: 2019919534

Print information available on the last page.

Any people depicted in stock imagery provided by Getty Images are models, and such images are being used for illustrative purposes only.
Certain stock imagery © Getty Images.

AMP
Scripture quotations marked AMP are from The Amplified Bible, Old Testament copyright © 1965, 1987 by the Zondervan Corporation. The Amplified Bible, New Testament copyright © 1954, 1958, 1987 by The Lockman Foundation. Used by permission. All rights reserved.

KJV
Scripture taken from The Holy Bible, King James Version. Public Domain

MSG
Scripture quotations marked MSG are taken from THE MESSAGE. Copyright © 1993, 1994, 1995, 1996, 2000, 2001, 2002, 2003 by Eugene H. Peterson. Used by permission of NavPress Publishing Group. Website.

NIV
Scripture quotations marked NIV are taken from the Holy Bible, New International Version®. NIV®. Copyright © 1973, 1978, 1984 by International Bible Society. Used by permission of Zondervan. All rights reserved. [Biblica]

ESV
Scripture quotations are from the ESV® Bible (The Holy Bible, English Standard Version®), copyright © 2001 by Crossway, a publishing ministry of Good News Publishers. Used by permission. All rights reserved.

This book is printed on acid-free paper.

Because of the dynamic nature of the Internet, any web addresses or links contained in this book may have changed since publication and may no longer be valid. The views expressed in this work are solely those of the author and do not necessarily reflect the views of the publisher, and the publisher hereby disclaims any responsibility for them.

CONTENTS

Dedication.. vii
Acknowledgments... xi

Chapter 1   The Marketplace 1
Chapter 2   Who Is The Uncommon Woman of Faith? 12
Chapter 3   What Are The Characteristics of An
            Uncommon Woman of Faith?.........................21
Chapter 4   What is The Kingdom of God?.......................32
Chapter 5   The Marketplace Revisited............................41
Chapter 6   God's Business Plan And Executive Summary...44
Chapter 7   The Marketplace Needs Laborers...................55
Chapter 8   The Juggernaut Prophecy.............................62
Chapter 9   Should I Tithe From My Business? 71
Chapter 10 Faith In The Marketplace 79
Chapter 11 We Can't Be Idle In The Marketplace..............84
Chapter 12 Success In The Marketplace..........................88
Chapter 13 Investment In The Marketplace......................91
Chapter 14 The Global Marketplace...............................95
Chapter 15 The Uncommon Business Woman Prayer
            of Faith 98

DEDICATION

It's customary to hear the term "ole school" if you're one to act or react in a manner that depicts you've been trained properly. I choose to render "schooled" because it's a component that today's society is missing. I want to honor those responsible for my being "schooled." Therefore, I dedicate this book to my parents James & Frances Johnson, who taught my siblings and I bootstrap mentality and love. Also, Grandma Sarah Thomas, who nurtured my spiritual growth until the age of five. There's nothing like family!

Secondarily, I dedicate this book to my brother James Johnson, Jr., whom I referred to as my big brother, although I'm the eldest. James, a godly and talented man with a powerful testimony of love who cared for many. His voice in song phenomenal and his stylish dress impeccable.

Thirdly, to my parents in love, Ralph & Dorothy Gibson, whose humor I love. The training of their only son Reginald, my husband, depicts godly and intellectual roots that can't be questioned. All of the parents mentioned above, and brother graduated to glory yet each left godly legacy.

I take this time to honor my children Tammie/Scott, Corey, ChaTea, Askia, and Selina. My dynamic, one of a kind, super talented siblings Leo/Valerie, Geraldine, Van/Dolores, Michelle/Bernial, and Tonya/Cornell. I cherish my grandchildren Brittany,

Noah, Scottie, Cam, Anfernee, Brandon, Cayleb, Asia, Talia, Ausar, Elijah, Castille, nephews and nieces and the princess, my great-grandchild Lane Michelle Fulton and her dad Dezmon Fulton.

I would be remised to overlook my Covenant Parents Bishop Keith A. Butler and his anointed and lovely wife, Pastor Deborah L. Butler. They nourished and poured into me the wisdom, knowledge, and understanding of the Gospel of Jesus Christ and the Kingdom of God. Their vital and strategic training in the areas of politics, issues of the day, and ministry start-up is invaluable. Also, the infamous Class of 93" Pistis School of Ministry. Special thanks to Dr. Stanley L. Scott and His ageless wife, Minister Carolyn Scott, who truly instilled a hunger for Christ in my life. Special acknowledgment to Attorney Jahan Berns and family. My genuine, powerful, and dynamic Ministers of Word of Faith Global Ministries, Inc, Birmingham, AL, who without them the vision would tarry.

My thanks to a man God is using tremendously in the sports industry, Mr. Tony Dungy. In 2010, my working engagement with him opened the revelation for my brand. Mr. Dungy autographed "To Uncommon Brandy" on his poster at Auburn University where he spoke to the Fellowship of Christian Athletes and Coaches. My brand at that moment became "UncommonBran" thanks to Holy Spirit. Special thanks to Darrin Gray, NFL and NBA clients and constituents.

To my dear friend and business ally Leigh Valentine, Pastor & Mrs. George Blanks, Bishop Willie Bradley, Pastor Gwen Bradley, Pastor Ray Cottrell & Pastor Rena' Cottrell. My dear sister in Christ and mentor Rev. Lucy McKee and her twin sister Re. Lynne Hammond, Dr. Billye Brim and my mentor Judge Jesse P. Slaton, who poured into me from Barbour Jr.

High, Detroit, MI. throughout my professional career until her departure from earth.

Special love to my European, African, India, and Israel team leaders and affiliates Minister Cadytema Dangbele and sons Kevin, Fabrice, Eric, Mbemba and their wives; Nicole Emany, Pastor Lucie Lupemba, Pastors Paul & Pauline Mahon, Marcelline Lukala, Minister Muriel Tephany, Pastors Bruno & Synphorose Kasonga, Bishop & Mrs. William Brown, Aniyshai Tshimanga, Minister & Mrs. Misha Emany, Mr. & Mrs. Lorise Emany, Pastors Jacob and Mary Mari, Ambassador Dr, Christine Niyonsavye, Julie Mukendi, Pastor Isaac Bosire, Rabbi Gershon Nduwa, Abraham Lincoln Bah, Douglas Okhostso and Ambassador Nonye Udo.

Lastly, my dearest supportive husband, Reginald, who affords me opportunity, support, and freedom to actively pursue God's plan for my life. The oneness we share is truly ordained by God, and I genuinely respect and love him dearly.

ACKNOWLEDGMENTS

"The book "Uncommon Woman of Faith in the Marketplace" is an invaluable contribution of Dr. Brandy F. Gibson to the empowerment of Christian women and the body of Christ at large, for the children of God to repossess "the mountains of industry" corrupted by the world system and make it available and proper to the Kingdom of God.

Dr. Brandy F. Gibson's tremendous skills in teaching, counseling and coaching are thoroughly displayed in this book, an eye-opener for Christians on God's business plan intended for them, on their true identity revealed in the word, on divine provision backing up every God-given dream or vision and on the Helper, the Holy Spirit, faithfully standing by their side.

This book is therefore a genuine roadmap for every child of God fed up with routine life in their comfort zone and earnestly willing and seeking to step into the destiny God designed for them."

Amb. Mahan Paul Nathanael
Head of Africa Department
Ministry of Foreign Affairs
Republic of Cote d'Ivoire

—⚏—

"The biblical principles shared by Dr. Gibson in this book will ignite your faith to continue to live a separated life and believe God for the possible."

Tonya Garner
Postmaster, Dearborn, MI

—♒—

"Dr Gibson's book The Uncommon Woman of Faith is an encouragement to consider mind renewal while pursuing purpose in the marketplace. The reader will be challenged and championed, to reflect God's glory as she implements the Heavenly Father's uncommon plan."

Min. Frankie Hing
Columbia, SC

—♒—

"Dr. Brandy definitely knows how to teach you to become an uncommon woman of faith in the marketplace. You will be blessed and reach a higher level in what God has called you to do as you read this amazing book."

Rev. Kate McVeigh
Evangelist/Author of The Blessing of Favor

—♒—

"If succeeding in business God's way is your purpose, this is a "Must Have"...

This book is a step-by-step empowering book for your business journey, which will enable you to build a successful kingdom grounded business.

As a believing woman, it will show you according to
God's approach your importance in the marketplace,
your uncommon business statutes in today's society, and
how to hear the secrets The Spirit of God is revealing
you concerning your business and field, in order for
you to be successful and build God's kingdom."

Rev. Pauline Mahan Gaithersburg, MD

"Over two thousand years ago the Apostle John
wrote, 'By this all people will know that you are my
disciples, if you have love for one another.' As a
follower of Christ you might wonder if such a concept
is possible in the cut-throat world of business. Gibson
persuasively makes the case that such concepts are
not only possible but a must for those who are seeking
to glorify God in their role as business women."

Darin W. White, Ph.D.
Chair, Entrepreneurship, Management, Marketing Department
Samford University, Birmingham, AL

"The Uncommon Woman of Faith In the Marketplace, by
Dr. Brandy F. Gibson, is not only a powerful book, but
life- changing! It's a great reminder that we as believers,
must walk in our God-given authority. By doing this,
it will cause us to thrive, achieve and prosper. It also
reveals that knowing who we are will not only propel

us to success, but it can also ignite a positive change in others, because of our godly focus and purpose."

LaTonya R. Jackson
Minister, Author
The Making Season, LLC

—*✦*—

"Too many Christians have been steered in the wrong direction as it pertains to their gifts, graces, and anointing, especially women. Born into a world where women are many times treated as second class citizens particularly in business and the work place. Many have set aside what God has created them to do, have put aside those plans and visions that God has given to be a blessing to a lost and dying world. In doing this many have moved away from the path of success and provision that has been ordained for them as they have fallen into the worldly trap of seeking all the things the Gentiles seek as well as doing it the world's way. It's time not only for women but all of God's people to reap what our Heavenly Father has prepared for us in our lives. The author of this book "Uncommon Woman of Faith in the Marketplace" has served in corporate America as the first African American female promoted to the Marketing Division of the US Postal Service, Detroit, Michigan and being promoted up the ranks. As an entrepreneur, business coach and a sought after speaker on this subject in the United States and throughout the world, Paris France, Brussels Belgium, Kinshasa DRC, Brandy F. Gibson is also Co-Pastor of Word of Faith Global Ministries and CEO of Lydia Joseph School of Business as well as my loving wife."

Reginald W. Gibson
Pastor, Word of Faith Global Ministries

—*✦*—

"This will be a great deposit and impartation to all who read! Life changing gems of business wisdom!"

Deb Campbell
Executive Director, DFZ

—⚬—

"I praise God for the timing of this book. As a woman of faith called to lead in the marketplace, this message is a shot in the arm, oxygen and encouragement to keep moving in the direction of my calling without fear but in total faith for what God can and will do through me, if I let him."

Michelle Mancha

—⚬—

"Dr. Brandy provides excellent guidance to anyone looking to fulfill their "God given" purpose. She empowers readers to reach their highest potential in entrepreneurship and life through Godly principles. This is a must read for anyone looking for next level blessing."

Shawn K. Brown
Host, Going the Distance w/Shawn Brown

—⚬—

"Great Kingdom information and principles for the Believer in the marketplace"

Angela Greene

—⚬—

"Dr Brandy Gibson's new book "The Uncommon Woman of Faith In the Marketplace" is a must read for women in business of any kind. Since I have been in the ministry, as well as a business coach after spending 14 years on QVC and TV Infommercials - I see the great need for this inspiring book. I am thrilled that Brandy is giving us incredible wisdom and scriptures on how to effectively change the atmosphere of every business and Entrepreneurship Endeavors. As women we all need this book! It will save us time, money and heartache.

After 3 decades, as a marketplace minister, I see that I still need to learn more on how to be truly successful for God's kingdom. Brandy's writings are encouraging me, to take it up to a higher level. To put my stake in the ground that I am not giving up or pulling back from the "Call of God" on my life and my business. God has a call on your life and according to Jeremiah 29:12 you must fulfill THE PLAN & PURPOSE on your life for this end time move. You are called! You are chosen! Read every scripture that Brandy has clearly laid out for you. You will GROW and GO onto new Heights bigger than ever before! You will PROSPER as you study these scriptures and the fresh revelation from Brandy's message. You will help the multitudes know the truth and lay up eternal rewards.

Trust me: You need to get a dozen of these books to give out all of your friends in marketplace ministry! God will bless you through Dr Brandy Gibson."

Leigh Valentine
CEO & Founder
Valentine Beauty Products.

CHAPTER ONE

THE MARKETPLACE

There are so many authors today writing about business-start-ups and/or improvement of current business practices. This book is similar yet profoundly different. As a female in business, you need assurances of entrepreneurial effectiveness. Your "how to" shouldn't outweigh your foundational applications towards your start-up or improving your business at its current capacity. Without a sure foundation, you're sure to collapse at some point. To initiate a company based off of someone's get-rich-quick scheme is ludicrous. This is an unreasonable and foolish approach to your business, as well as your name.

The so-called get-rich-quick methods only benefit the initiator of the program and not you. There are valuable and legitimate coaching and instructional programs to assist you in your business endeavors, but you must discern, which is relevant or invaluable to you. Marketing platforms geared to you becoming wealthy overnight should generate a yellow light of caution. As a disclaimer, there are some excellent marketing platforms for business start-ups, but discernment is vital in determining what's best for you.

This book informs you why you need to pursue your business and fulfilling your purpose in this season. To accomplish anything in life, relationships are crucial to obtaining fulfillment. Building a support team is advantageous because they help you in the process of planning your goals and timelines. Your support team should always bring something to the table and not act as cookie cutters. A cookie-cutter team player will be very traditional in a high level of predictability. You need someone that will challenge your goals and provide you with strategic alternatives for you and your business. You don't need average when you're called to soar in life. Flying below the radar will give you the same designed response every time.

This season of mankind is very unique in nature because it's the season for the Body of Christ to arise and excel in repossessing the mountains of industry back into the Kingdom of God. God never intended that the Body of Christ lack in anything. So, to initiate your God-given dream and pursue your business start-up, you must act in faith by rising to action. God's glory upon you will attract wealth and riches on your behalf.

Isaiah 60:1-3-ESV - *Arise, shine, for your light has come, and the glory of the Lord has risen upon you. For behold, darkness shall cover the earth, and thick darkness the peoples; but the Lord will arise upon you, and His glory will be seen upon you. And nations shall come to your light, and kings to the brightness of your rising.*

Prophetically for some, it is more vital for you to build wealth streams than relationships because of what is preceding us in this season of time. These individuals need to go after their heritage. (This Word of prophecy was recently given by Rabbi Curt Landry).

Isaiah 60:4-5 - KJV - *Lift up thine eyes round about, and see: all they gather themselves together, they come to thee: thy sons shall come from far, and thy daughters shall be nursed at thy* *side. Then thou shalt see, and flow together, and thine heart shall fear, and be enlarged; because the abundance of the sea shall be converted unto thee, the forces of the Gentiles shall come unto thee.*

God needs us in the marketplace because there we find the world in need of a Savior. There we find the medium of exchange to transact business and exist in this temporal system. We need financial wealth to further the Kingdom of God because third world nations require clean water, vegetation, medical facilities, education, housing, nurturing, and training for widows and orphans, and much more. Greed will not meet the needs of mankind, only a loving God through His Kingdom citizens.

Today, there's a rise in the marketplace among believers who are applying their business acumen and personal skill-set toward kingdom purpose. Entire nations are being shaken with believers aware of promoting the Kingdom of God. It's His Kingdom, so it must be done in His way of doing things in the marketplace. Corporate America has been utilizing the dominative business plan that God decreed at the Beginning of Creation. Capitalism has applied God's formula for centuries, while the Church hast slept God's principles and laws of the Kingdom. Why is that? One viable reason is the institution of religion that goes against God's Kingdom plans and implements its own. Religion doesn't comprehend God's Kingdom on earth. To them it's in the sweet by and by when we all get to heaven.

Matthew 6:7-10 -KJV - *But when ye pray, use not vain repetitions, as the heathen do: for they think that they shall be heard for their much speaking. Be not ye therefore like unto them: for your Father knoweth what things ye have need of, before ye ask him. After this manner therefore pray ye: Our Father which art in heaven, Hallowed be thy name. **Thy Kingdom come. Thy will be done in earth, as it is in heaven.***

God's business plan is derived from Genesis 1:28. His Word cannot return unto Him void of action, power, or fruit-bearing. It's time to obtain knowledge and renew our minds to the practical use of this plan and apply it to the God-given dream for your business. When God gives you an idea or a vision within you, He also makes provision for it. Your part is to receive His Word, believe it, and act upon it in faith. Whatever door He opens for you, no man can shut, and whatever door He shuts, no man can open. He has spoken, so shall He do it.

Isaiah 55:9-10 - *For as the rain cometh down, and the snow from heaven, and returneth not thither, but watereth the earth, and maketh it bring forth and bud, that it may give seed to the sower, and bread to the eater: So shall my Word be that goeth forth out of my mouth:it shall not return unto me void, but it shall accomplish that which I please, and it shall prosper in the thing whereto I sent it.*

Women today are shaking the marketplace like never before. Barriers of yesteryear are being destroyed, and glass ceilings smashed to smithereens. The women of God have seen and heard within their hearts their designated purpose. The problem with this excellent, groundbreaking momentum is that women of the world don't realize that it's time for the big payback, and they're oblivious to how to obtain and whom to obtain it from. They don't have an ear to hear what The Spirit of God is saying; this gives the uncommon woman of faith in the marketplace the advantage to soar and influence many.

The common woman is pursuing the inadequate and degrading means of obtaining wealth and promotion through carnal applications. Using her body negatively, she advances towards achieving promotion by seeing more ceilings than Michaelangelo. Upon an ill-gotten gain, she boasts of her position and hoards her wealth because she fears it will flee from her.

An uncommon woman won't hoard profits but provides employment for those in need. She promotes training and evangelizing the world. At this juncture, the woman of faith is now called out of the cave she's been hiding in. Your dreams will become realities without doubting its feasibility. God has spoken and your fear of failure is not optional. You can't give excuses in preventing your business start-up. Don't allow fear to hinder your pursuit of obtaining God's best for you. Your Beginning is knowing who you are in Christ. It's in Him you move, achieve, excel, and have your being.

Acts 17:28 - *For in Him we live, and move, and have our being; as certain also of your own poets have said, For we are also His offspring.*

Your initial approach is to know the purpose of God and His business plan for marketplace achievement. This is the objective of this book. Knowing God's purpose for the marketplace and how to implement what He originated in the Beginning will give you the confidence and success you need. Your engagement towards jump-starting your business or improving your business is to know who you are and to see yourself in the manner God sees you. He doesn't see you fearful, nor defeated. You are not the common businesswoman of today's society. God has made you uncommon and will exalt you up unexpectedly. The problem with most Christians in the business arena is the issue of identity and authority.

I Corinthians 1:30- KJV - *But of him are ye in Christ Jesus, who of God is made unto us wisdom, and righteousness, and sanctification, and redemption: That, according as it is written, He that glorieth, let him glory in the Lord.*

This is why Genesis 1:28 is invaluable for you.

Genesis 1:27-28 - *So God created man in his own image, in the image of God created he him; male and female created he them. And God blessed them, and God said unto them, Be fruitful, and multiply, and replenish the earth, and subdue it: and have dominion over the fish of the sea, and over the fowl of the air, and over every living thing that moveth upon the earth.*

How are you viewing yourself? What image are you attempting to pattern? We will cover God's business plan in detail later in another chapter. Presently, let's focus on you being the unique masterpiece He created and know there's only one you in the history of creation and you're made in His image. Look in the mirror right now and see the uniqueness you possess. You're uniquely and wonderfully made. Now read the following aloud.

Psalms 139:1-3 - *O Lord, thou hast searched me, and known me. Thou knowest my downsitting and mine uprising, thou understandest my thought afar off. Thou compassest my path and my lying down, and art acquainted with all my ways.*

Look at verse 13 and 14:

For thou hast possessed my reins: thou hast covered me in my mother's womb. I will praise thee; for I am fearfully and wonderfully made: marvellous are thy works; and that my soul knoweth right well. My substance was not hid from thee, when I was made in secret, and curiously wrought in the lowest parts of the earth. Thine eyes did see my substance, yet being unperfect; and in thy book all my members were written, which in continuance were fashioned, when as yet there was none of them. How precious also are thy thoughts unto me, O God!

Now, return back to the mirror and take a more in-depth look at yourself based on what you just read and precisely what God has said about you. Take time out to read all of Psalms 139 for your further empowerment and enrichment.

Now, let's make a comparison of your invaluable worth. Before reading the Word of God, some of you didn't have self-assurance earlier. From reading God's Word, true empowerment surged within you that enables you to excel in whatever your heart desires. So, think about it - the more you read from God's Word seeing yourself in it will edify you. Your confidence factor bombards every facet of fear that tries to say you're unable to achieve anything, especially starting a business.

The cliche which had some merit before today is now passe states most businesses fail in the first five years. You and I are in Christ, and in Him, we cannot fail. It doesn't mean you won't make a mistake or two. Mistakes are what you learn from. What is failure? Failure is being unsuccessful in achieving your goals. Failure is a rejection to do or achieve something. You have actually made a decision to quit; that's an actual failure. Now let's look at what a mistake is.

A mistake is an action that is misguided or wrong. So, pursue your God-given dream and purpose by following the Holy Spirit's leading. He doesn't operate in failure or mistakes. If you make a mistake, go back to the drawing board, regroup, strategize, downsize, do whatever is necessary to correct the error.

Too often, Christians assume God will bless their endeavors based on their salvation merits. In other words, "I'm saved, and that's enough." They apply themselves to fulfilling their hearts desire without seeking God. The reading of His Word with prayer and meditation of the Word gives guidance. They engage in endeavors they're not called to, so the possibilities of experiencing roadblocks, negative feedback, and even failure is inevitable. This is due to a mind over matter approach and listening to the wrong voices. You may have listened to what your parents said you were to do in life, and you became what mom or dad wanted you to pursue. These are wrong actions with good intentions. You must seek God regarding your purpose here on earth.

If you're one who has listened to the demands of a loving parent who only wanted the best for you or they may have wanted to vicariously live their life through you because they missed their opportunity vocationally, you've found it hard to live with. You regret going to work or working the family business, and it becomes complicated for you. You try getting through the day because you know there's something else that can bring you joy and fulfillment. This is why you experience "Blue Monday," and you go into survival mode, which affects your entire week. There's a lack of creativity in operation only daydreaming of what you really want to do, and you're living for the weekend. You're also living for the paycheck, which means you're chasing money. Money flees when it is pursued.

Your parents' assignment or your friend's career suggestion is not your assignment. You must seek God for your answers in life. There's nothing magical with God, nor with you when you've received His Son Jesus to pattern yourself by.

Let's look at the standard practices of the world in business. By far, it can't compare to the Kingdom of God because everything in the earth called trade has been twisted by satan, who always tries to duplicate God. The enemy (satan) doesn't have an original idea at all.

There are no self-made millionaires or billionaires. Everything exists in God, Who gave us Biblical principles in the earth.

The world has operated in these principles and prospered in doing so.

Here's a simple example: The mafia would give money in large quantities to the church, and they received from their seed sown. Whether good or bad, a person gains. It's a law. What you sow you also reap, but overall, the church has refrained from sowing and wonders why God hasn't blessed them financially. Instead of tithing and giving, they refrain from either due to a bill they chose to pay. They override the prompting of the Holy Spirit's unction to be a blessing.

Ecclesiastes 11:4 - *He that observeth the wind shall not sow; and he that regardeth the clouds shall not reap. (King James Version)*

Matthew 6:26 -28 - *Behold the fowls of the air: for they sow not, neither do they reap, nor gather into barns; yet your heavenly Father feedeth them. Are ye not much better than they? Which of you by taking thought can add one cubit unto his stature? And why take ye thought for raiment? Consider the lilies of the field, how they grow; they toil not, neither do they spin:*

Luke 12:24 - *Consider the ravens: for they neither sow nor reap; which neither have storehouse nor barn; and God feedeth them: how much more are ye better than the fowls?*

John 10:10 - *The thief cometh not, but for to steal, and to kill, and to destroy: I am come that they might have life, and that they might have it more abundantly.*

God is in the business of kingdom expansion, and that means He must be in every sphere of day to day marketplace. Religion and traditionalism won't fit into God's scheme of things in His Kingdom. We are to become the kingdom's influence on the earth in sports, arts, science, communications, technology, politics, education, business, and more. God should see us on assignment in possessing the world for His kingdom plan. We, as women today, are called out to expand God's Kingdom on earth.

Isaiah 54:1-6 - KJV - *Sing, O barren, thou that didst not bear; break forth into singing, and cry aloud, thou that didst not travail with child: for more are the children of the desolate than the children of the married wife, saith the Lord. Enlarge the place of thy tent, and let them stretch forth the curtains of thine habitations: spare not, lengthen thy cords, and strengthen thy stakes; For thou shalt break forth on the right hand and on the left; and thy seed shall inherit the Gentiles, and make the desolate cities to be inhabited. Fear not; for thou shalt not be ashamed: neither be thou confounded; for thou shalt not be put to shame: for thou shalt forget the shame of thy youth, and shalt not remember the reproach of thy widowhood any more. For thy Maker is thine husband; the Lord of hosts is His name; and thy Redeemer the Holy One of Israel; The God of the whole earth shall he be called. For the Lord hath called thee as a woman forsaken and grieved in spirit, and a wife of youth, when thou wast refused, saith thy God.*

Kingdom expansion doesn't mean throwing away the doctrines of the church and settling for a placebo type church that makes you feel good and is void of responsibility. Placebo styled ministries allow you to hear a motivating speech and have fun fellowshipping with each other, yet you're not challenged to be accountable to God's Word. This is a subtle move of the enemy (satan). There's absolutely nothing wrong with fellowship and motivation, but Jesus said "Teach and make disciples;"

The primary emphasis is that we're to be like Christ Jesus. To do so means we must do what He did, spend time with His

Heavenly Father, to obtain His Plan and start your day. Jesus, while on earth, was teaching and preaching, healing the sick, and living the Kingdom of God. We can do the same in our business climates. Allow me to clarify doing what Jesus did. Everything that God does He does in order. Therefore, when hired in the marketplace and you engage company time by spending time on the internet for personal use that's stealing. Personal phone calls on company time is literally stealing. Stealing company resources such as paper clips, pens, pencils, notepads, or other items are inevitably stealing.

To teach and preach in the marketplace should be your lifestyle before, man. To heal in the market is your attitude displayed before others. In addition to your lifestyle and attitude is the fact that you can literally preach and teach verbally, tangibly lay hands on the sick and they shall recover on your lunch or break time. That's orderly kingdom business.

GEMS: Every great dream begins with a dreamer. Always remember, you have within you the strength, the patience, and the passion to reach for the stars to change the world. -**Harriet Tubman**

CHAPTER TWO

WHO IS THE UNCOMMON WOMAN OF FAITH?

In II John Chapter one, we read of the Apostle John speaking highly of the elect lady and of her children. He's warning the elect lady against false teachers. He exhorts her and her family to continue to love one another being conscientious against deceivers. John cautions them to stand for the truth, the truth they heard in the beginning. Ironically we're dealing with the same factor today but of more intensity.

We can view this the elect lady as the nation of Israel, but for the sake of current times, I'm elaborating regarding the modern woman of today. This woman in John's day was a woman of phenomenal influence that's quite impressive. The importance of a godly nature should be every woman's caveat and the epitome of every woman of God to become. Being a caveat is being a woman who prevents injustices like Harriet Tubman. Such crimes like human trafficking, abortion, abusing the poor, children, and the elderly. Let's face it, being influential affords us the opportunity and power from God to affect someone or something by our godly character and applied actions.

An influential woman has the power to cause change without directly forcing change by manipulation. To exercise manipulation and negative influence embodies the potential or capacity to cause corrupt interference for personal gain. This is also a form of witchcraft in operation.

Obviously, this was not the elect lady in II John chapter one. The word **elect** here in Greek is eklektos (Pronounced ek-lek-tos'), meaning favorite, chosen, picked out, the best of its kind or class, excellence, preeminence that's applied to a specific individual means chosen by God; to obtain salvation through Christ.

Christians are called out or chosen by God. Although called out or adopted, it's our decision to accept or reject the call. God never forces anyone to take Him or His calling.

The Messiah was called **"elect"** and appointed by God to the most exalted office conceivable. Now, imagine these attributes upon you His uncommon, favorite, classy, saved, chosen, and the best in your industry or culture, a woman of influence because we're made in His image.

Notice in II John 1:4-6, the elect lady's children were blessed and walking in the truth. In verse 13, we see her sister was elect as well. Two elect sisters and their children were walking in the truth. Neither of them is relying on the school system to teach and train their children the truth. This is a heritage of the Lord.

The synonym for influential is authority, the ability to impress, affect, sway, or touch one's life. God needs this woman today to execute a positive and powerful influence on the earth that epitomizes the Kingdom of God on earth. The uncommon woman operates in a manner totally opposite of a woman of the world or a religious woman in a chaotic world gone mad focused on self-indulgence, greed, and sin.

To be the common woman is to express and live out an anti-God lifestyle in sin and verbally express your right to do so. There's a boldness in their foul alternative style of living and without regard to an offense. What's interesting is the marketing media campaigns that operate on their behalf, expressing a worldly sense of dominance in their style of living when, in reality, only ten percent of the population claim this status. As Christians, we should become even bolder and more assertive in expressing our God-given citizenship on earth and the exemplary freedom it warrants.

Acts 18:9b - NIV - *"Do not be afraid; keep on speaking, do not be silent."*

The world is full of customized ideologies and philosophical beliefs that go against God's Word. This appears to be glamorized, and the world enjoys jumping on the bandwagon of carnality. The appearance of the sin nature is the way to go for the world, but not so! Media hype illustrates these views in their televised news broadcasts, movies, television dramas, comedy shows, and social media. It's geared for acceptance of this commonality that is desensitized and targeted as the norm of today's society. It's magnified towards our children, the next generation.

When something is magnified, it's because it's small in a measure, less than desirable to see. Don't be deceived the Apostle John says to the Elect Lady of influence and power. To be conventional means to fall below ordinary standards and lacks refinement. Refinement is the process of improving or making something pure. Can you genuinely say that this is today's common factor?

Galatians 6:7 - KJV - *Be not deceived God is not mocked; whatsoever a man soweth, that shall he also reap.*

As influential women of faith, we are privy to possessing the ability to create God's Kingdom environment based on the Word of God into our marketplace. We make it conducive by maintaining fellowship with Holy Spirit Who leads, guides, directs, helps, comforts, and is a constant standby and an advocate when needed. We should always consult Him in all matters. By habitually doing this, the ease of operation in life and business is sweatless. This is not to say that issues won't arise, and adversity comes your way; it's to say that Holy Spirit advocates the matters and problems you face because you place Him and God's Word first.

Being uncommon is being extraordinaire, phenomenal, and unique. You explode with creativity in ministry, business, family, finances through wisdom, knowledge, and understanding of the Word of God and of your area of expertise. Being rare and uncommon affords you favor. You operate like this because God has bestowed it upon you.

Proverbs 31:13-31-KJV - *She seeketh wool, and flax, and worketh willingly with her hands. She is like the merchants' ships; she bringeth her food from afar. She riseth also while it is yet night, and giveth meat to her household, and a portion to her maidens. She considereth a field, and buyeth it: with the fruit of her hands she planteth a vineyard. She girdeth her loins with strength, and strengtheneth her arms. She perceiveth that her merchandise is good: her candle goeth not out by night. She layeth her hands to the spindle, and her hands hold the distaff. She stretcheth out her hand to the poor; yea, she reacheth forth her hands to the needy. She is not afraid of the snow for her household: for all her household are clothed with scarlet. She maketh herself coverings of tapestry; her clothing is silk and purple. Her husband is known in the gates, when he sitteth among the elders of the land. She maketh fine linen, and selleth it; and delivereth girdles unto the merchant.*

Strength and honour are her clothing; and she shall rejoice in time to come. She openeth her mouth with wisdom; and in her tongue is the law of kindness. She looketh well to the ways of her household, and eateth not the bread of idleness. Her children arise up, and call her blessed; her husband also, and he praiseth her. Many daughters have done virtuously, but thou excellest them all. Favour is deceitful, and beauty is vain: but a woman that feareth the Lord, she shall be praised. Give her of the fruit of her hands; and let her own works praise her in the gates.

Proverbs 10:22 - KJV *-The Blessing of the Lord, it maketh rich, and He addeth no sorrow with it.*

The word **"sorrow"** in Proverbs 10:22 in Hebrew is defined toiling. You and I are not called to toil. We're called to manage and dominate. When God gives you vision or dreams for business or ministry, there's never a competition. You don't compete with the vision given you. You fulfill the vision because every resource, client, customer, and more have been provided. The responsibility you have is to manage what was given you. By walking out your business vision and adhering to Holy Spirit, you become the head and not the tail, and everyone is trying to compete with you. Today's example is Chick Fil A. You are to enjoy the Blessing!

Daniel 1:20 - ASV *- And in every matter of wisdom and understanding, concerning which the king inquired of them, he found them ten times better than all the magicians and enchanters that were in all his realm.*

Let's view how Daniel handled his uncommon character in a trying situation among the worldly heathen in his time.

Daniel 2: 1-11-KJV - *And in the second year of the reign of Nebuchadnezzar Nebuchadnezzar dreamed dreams, wherewith his spirit was troubled, and his sleep brake from him. Then the king commanded to call the magicians, and the astrologers, and the sorcerers, and the Chaldeans, for to shew the king his dreams. So they came and stood before the king. And the king said unto them, I have dreamed a dream, and my spirit was troubled to know the dream. Then spake the Chaldeans to the king in Syriack, O king, live for ever: tell thy servants the dream, and we will shew the interpretation. The king answered and said to the Chaldeans, The thing is gone from me: if ye will not make known unto me the dream, with the interpretation thereof, ye shall be cut in pieces, and your houses shall be made a dunghill. But if ye shew the dream, and the interpretation thereof, ye shall receive of me gifts and rewards and great honour: therefore shew me the dream, and the interpretation thereof. They answered again and said, Let the king tell his servants the dream, and we will shew the interpretation of it. The king answered and said, I know of certainty that ye would gain the time, because ye see the thing is gone from me. But if ye will not make known unto me the dream, there is but one decree for you: for ye have prepared lying and corrupt words to speak before me, till the time be changed: therefore tell me the dream, and I shall know that ye can shew me the interpretation thereof. The Chaldeans answered before the king, and said, There is not a man upon the earth that can shew the king's matter: therefore there is no king, Lord, nor ruler, that asked such things at any magician, or astrologer, or Chaldean. And it is a **rare thing** that the king requireth, and there is none other that can shew it before the king, except the gods, whose dwelling is not with flesh.*

The Hebrew word **rare** in verse eleven is yaqqiyr pronounced "yak-keer" meaning noble, famous, difficult. What the Chaldean soothsayers were saying is that this capability is uncommon in our world today. The Chaldeans magicians, soothsayers, and astrologers at this time were of a certain order and wore a peculiar dress like that seen of the gods, which were of Aramean decent. Because of their reply to the king he became very angry and petitioned for their execution. Look at verse nineteen:

Daniel 2:19-30 - KJV - *Then was the secret revealed unto Daniel in a night vision. Then Daniel blessed the God of heaven. Daniel answered and said, Blessed be the name of God for ever and ever: for wisdom and might are his: And He changeth the times and the seasons: He removeth kings, and setteth up kings: He giveth wisdom unto the wise, and knowledge to them that know understanding: He revealeth the deep and secret things: He knoweth what is in the darkness, and the light dwelleth with Him. I thank thee, and praise thee, O thou God of my fathers, who hast given me wisdom and might, and hast made known unto me now what we desired of thee: for Thou hast now made known unto us the king's matter. Therefore Daniel went in unto Arioch, whom the king had ordained to destroy the wise men of Babylon: he went and said thus unto him; Destroy not the wise men of Babylon: bring me in before the king, and I will shew unto the king the interpretation. Then Arioch brought in Daniel before the king in haste, and said thus unto him, I have found a man of the captives of Judah, that will make known unto the king the interpretation. The king answered and said to Daniel, whose name was Belteshazzar, Art thou able to make known unto me the dream which I have seen, and the interpretation thereof? Daniel answered in the presence of the king, and said, The secret which the king hath demanded cannot the wise men, the astrologers, the magicians, the soothsayers, shew unto the king; But there is a God in heaven that revealeth secrets, and maketh known to the king Nebuchadnezzar what shall be in the latter days. Thy dream, and the visions of thy head upon thy bed, are these; As for thee, O king, thy thoughts came into thy mind upon thy* *bed, what should come to pass hereafter: and he that revealeth secrets maketh known to thee what shall come to pass. But as for me, this secret is not revealed to me for any wisdom that I have more than any living, but for their sakes that shall make known the interpretation to the king, and that thou mightest know the thoughts of thy heart.*

We see clearly from Scripture that this **"rare"** thing is displayed by Daniel from God. Daniel is seen having favor with God and man (Arioch) and he flowed with insight from God. Notice, Daniel was granted time to pray with his friends to petition and hear from God for the interpretation of the dream, the soothsayers weren't allotted such. So God granted Daniel wisdom and revelation to answer the king, that's favor being granted. Daniel had to have uncommon faith in approaching Arioch because he was the king's executioner. If Daniel failed, he was a dead man.

Daniel 2:24-KJV - *Therefore Daniel went in unto Arioch, whom the king had ordained to destroy the wise men of Babylon: he went and said thus unto him; Destroy not the wise men of Babylon: bring me in before the king, and I will shew unto the king the interpretation.*

God is a revealer of secrets, and this comes by having consistent fellowship with God. Your business is a day to day operation that demands excellence to excel. Sustainability is mediocre in today's gamut of the marketplace. It's all in you, and your time with Holy Spirit will bring forth hidden business strategies on your behalf and so much more.

Doors that were closed to you will supernaturally open because of insights from God that provide you direction. Favor will rest upon you like a coat of colors, all will see it and you. Favor rested upon Joseph, whose title under Pharaoh meant revealer of secrets. We must have insight from God to execute His plans and strategies. We must also give Him all the glory for what He's doing in our lives. There's no way you nor I could accomplish the plan given us unless the Creator of the plan gave it to us.

Jeremiah 33:3 - KJV - *Call unto me, and I will answer thee, and shew thee great and mighty things, which thou knowest not*

Call to Me and I will answer you, and will tell you great and mighty things, things hidden that you have not known.

Amos 4:13- ESV - *For behold, he who forms the mountains and creates the wind, and declares to man what is His thought, who makes the morning darkness, and treads on the heights of the earth— the Lord, the God of hosts, is His name!*

Holy Spirit will inform us of mapping out our businesses and our futures. He will not place us in positions of becoming workaholics that go against our body designed functions. God designed us as unique masterpieces without load-bearing features. Even the camel has his loads removed.

Matthew 19:23-24 ASV - *And Jesus said unto His disciples, Verily I say unto you, It is hard for a rich man to enter into the kingdom of heaven. And again I say unto you, It is easier for a camel to go through a needle's eye, than for a rich man to enter into the kingdom of God.*

On an average, a rich man or woman depend and have faith in their riches and not in God. Greed and sin follow such character, and hell becomes a destination. We can't allow that burden to be placed upon us who are godly entrepreneurs.

GEMS: It's not the load that breaks you down, it's the way you carry it. **- Lena Horne**

CHAPTER THREE

WHAT ARE THE CHARACTERISTICS OF AN UNCOMMON WOMAN OF FAITH?

The word "common" in retrospect to being God's uncommon woman highlights the world's view of today's women who are contrary to the Word of God. So, what's common and what's uncommon? Let's be clear regarding what side of the spectrum common and uncommon are operating in?

Jesus gave us the commandment to love. The world's common expression of love is twisted. Their acceptance and defilement of the true meaning is a total contradiction to the commandment of Jesus. The typical appearance of love in the world is lust. Lust has replaced true love in every temporal aspect. Lust has become the world's common.

John 13:34 – *A new commandment I give unto you; That ye love one another, as I have loved you, that ye also love one another. King James Version*

When the world critiques a significant corporation, its CEO, and its global expansion, people applaud their efforts. They glamorize the CEO's jet, his or her mansions lived in by justifiable earnings and feel it's okay that they operate with such status. The highest office or vocation on earth is a minister of Jesus Christ. Today, the world tries to de-value this profession. True love in operation would make sure the men and women of God, their ministries, and teams have all the accommodations necessary to save souls, feed families, heal the sick, and teach a nation. This would be engaged upon by financially supporting their efforts from their personal and business coffers. True love is the answer, but the secular view is, "What's love got to do with it?"

The character of a common worldly woman is one of ill-nature and void of true love. Because of this vacuum within she settles for anything and the message of failure they bring. She adapts a silly acceptance of achievement by any means necessary, and her business practices are conniving geared towards envy and destruction. She's the type of woman who is continually attending business conferences with an anti-god view and donates excessive amounts of money to organizations that are anti-god. She's the hunter that gets captured by the game.

II Timothy 4:3-4 - *For the time will come when they will not endure sound doctrine; but after their own lusts shall they heap to themselves teachers, having itching ears; 4-And they shall turn away their ears from the truth, and shall be turned unto fables.*

II Timothy 3:1-7-ASV - *But know this, that in the last days grievous times shall come. For men shall be lovers of self, lovers of money, boastful, haughty, railers, disobedient to parents,* unthankful, unholy, without natural affection, implacable, slanderers, without self-control, fierce, no lovers of good, traitors, headstrong, puffed up, lovers of pleasure rather than lovers of God; holding a form of godliness, but having denied the power thereof: from these also turn away. For of these are they that creep into houses, and take captive silly women laden with sins, led away by divers lusts, ever learning, and never able to come to the knowledge of the truth. We as believers should exercise our influence upon others in order to win the world for Jesus Christ. We have been given the authority and ability to navigate our influence.

GEMS: "To remain neutral in the use of our influence is to surrender our spiritual, moral and physical power over the enemy." *- Bishop Ronald Chipp*

As a powerful, influential woman of faith, we demonstrate our prowess in glorifying God in business. We can't become mobilized by peer pressure or worldly elements. Peer pressure can be fear that prevents us from taking the leap of faith in business as well as life. Becoming politically correct instead of Biblically correct stagnates godly influence. Our influence must continually be used to advance the Kingdom of God.

The defining moment in making decisions towards whether to execute positive or negative influence in one's life. Today's influential woman should be revealed to epitomize the Kingdom of God and operate uncommonly in a common chaotic world focused on self- indulgence, greed, and sin. The extraordinary woman of faith speaks boldly in her industry and community. She is God's advertising mouthpiece.

Acts 18:9b - Amplified Version— *One night the Master spoke to Paul in a dream: "Keep it up, and don't let anyone intimidate or silence you."*

John 4:34-38 - *Jesus saith unto them, My meat is to do the will of Him that sent Me, and to finish His work. Say not ye, There are yet four months, and then cometh harvest? behold, I say unto you, Lift up your eyes, and look on the fields; for they are white already to harvest. And he that reapeth receiveth wages, and gathereth fruit unto life eternal: that both he that soweth and he that reapeth may rejoice together. And herein is that saying true, One soweth, and another reapeth. I sent you to reap that whereon ye bestowed no labour: other men laboured, and ye are entered into their labours.*

Micah 4:13 (MSG) *On your feet, Daughter of Zion! Be threshed of chaff, be refined of dross. I'm remaking you into a people invincible, into God's juggernaut to crush the godless peoples. You'll bring their plunder as holy offerings to God, their wealth to the Master of the earth.*

There's a vast gulf of difference between women of the world and Christian women of faith. The obvious answer is the light and darkness issue and the infamous gift of revealed knowledge accessible to the woman of faith. Why? Because she has a relationship with God, The Father of all creation through Jesus Christ. So, why the marketplace issue? Simple, the era of waffling between two worlds is over. It's over because the fullness of time is ever so near, and the enormous gap has narrowed itself, meaning the line has been drawn in the sand. Either you're on the Lord's side serving Him and His Kingdom, or you're in the world's system serving satan in his defeated order of lack, failure, death, and an eternal lake of fire abode. Business is directed for profit, gain, a life worth living in abundance, and God wants you to have it now, not upon your arrival in heaven.

We must understand that God's economic systems are being executed by those outsides of the church, and the church wants to get upset about it. We can't, we have the same playing field. To try and divide the rich from the poor is a political application of division that we shouldn't partake of. So, what are we doing wrong? It's managing. When God created Adam, He created him to have dominion and to manage His creation.

Genesis 1:26 - 31 KJV - *And God said, Let us make man in our image, after our likeness: and let them have dominion over the fish of the sea, and over the birds of the heavens, and over the cattle, and over all the earth, and over every creeping thing that creepeth upon the earth. And God created man in his own image, in the image of God created he him; male and female created he them. And God blessed them: and God said unto them, Be fruitful, and multiply, and replenish the earth, and subdue it; and have dominion over the fish of the sea, and over the birds of the heavens, and over every living thing that moveth upon the earth. And God said, Behold, I have given you every herb yielding seed, which is upon the face of all the earth, and every tree, in which is the fruit of a tree yielding seed; to you it shall be for food: and to every beast of the earth, and to every bird of the heavens, and to everything that creepeth upon the earth, wherein there is life, I have given every green herb for food: and it was so. And God saw everything that he had made, and, behold, it was very good.*

Everything God made was and is excellent. Whatever God gives you is to be in the same manner, good. Good is to be desired or approved of and having the qualities of a particular role. So, God has placed inside you everything you need to prosper and be in health. How does it manifest? By your fellowship with God through the study of His Word, worshipping Him, and managing what He has given you. Management is key.

Matthew 25:21- ESV- *His Master said to him, 'Well done, good and faithful servant. You have been faithful over a little; I will set you over much. Enter into the joy of your Master.*

Manage what you have, whether large or small it boils down to your faithfulness and love. So, you're managing the little things, your minimum wage job, you're tithing the tenth, and giving offerings into the Kingdom God with a joyful heart.

Luke 9:38-KJV - *Give, and it shall be given unto you; good measure, pressed down, and shaken together, and running over, shall men give into your bosom. For with the same measure that ye mete withal it shall be measured to you again*

II Corinthians 9:6-12-KJV - *But this I say, He which soweth sparingly shall reap also sparingly; and he which soweth bountifully shall reap also bountifully. Every man according as he purposeth in his heart, so let him give; not grudgingly, or of necessity: for God loveth a cheerful giver. And God is able to make all grace abound toward you; that ye, always having all sufficiency in all things, may abound to every good work: (As it is written, He hath dispersed abroad; he hath given to the poor: his righteousness remaineth for ever. Now he that ministereth seed to the sower both minister bread for your food, and multiply your seed sown, and increase the fruits of your righteousness;) Being enriched in every thing to all bountifulness, which causeth through us thanksgiving to God. For the administration of this service not only supplieth the want of the saints, but is abundant also by many thanksgivings unto God;*

Your giving must not be in vain or reluctantly. Your expectation is based on your heart of love. The return on your giving is not always in the form of money which so many believers look for.

What's in your heart to fulfill in life regarding business is met by your spirit of giving.

Why is it taking so long to arrive? Because of your management, expectancy, and your heart of belief. Could it be what you're speaking?

Proverbs 18:21 – God's Word Version - *The tongue has the power of life and death, and those who love to talk will have to eat their own words.*

Matthew 12:34: *34You children of serpents! How can you say anything good when you are evil? For the mouth speaks out of the abundance of the heart. 35A good person brings good things out of a good treasure, and an evil person brings evil things out of an evil treasure. 36I tell you, on the day of judgment people will give an account for every thoughtless word they utter. 37For by your words you will be acquitted, and by your words you will be condemned."*

We hear so often celebrities at awards events giving glory and honor to God and immediately following they're blurting out profanity that's applauded and leaves an adolescent thinking it's okay to operate in this manner because they have swag.

God's word is clear:

James 3:10-11- ISV – *Out of the same mouth proceedeth blessing and cursing. My brethren these things ought not so to be. 11.Doth a fountain send forth at the same place sweet water and bitter?*

Ephesians 4:29 – *Let not corrupt communication proceed out of your mouth, but that which is good to the use of edifying, that it may minister grace unto the hearers.*

Swag and Swagger

Let's deal with the familiar word of the day, "swag or swagger." This word rings from the pulpit to the pit, decreeing allegedly a demeanor of classy style, a persona of fresh, well dressed savvy. But quite the contrary. Let's look at the definition.

Swag - *noun*

a curtain or piece of fabric fastened so as to hang in a drooping curve.
a decorative garland or chain of flowers, foliage, or fruit fastened so as to hang in a drooping curve.
plural noun: **swags**
"swags of holly and mistletoe"
a carved or painted representation of a swag of flowers, foliage, or fruit.
"fine plaster swags"
informal
money or goods taken by a thief or burglar. "their homes offer tempting swag for burglars"
products given away free, typically for promotional purposes. "local studios provide swag, spirits, and food"
US marijuana, typically of a low grade.
"prices range from $40 a 10-seed packet for some Jamaican swag to $345 per pack for something tastier"
***Obtained from Google Search dictionary.*

Swagger:

DEFINITION OF SWAGGER

intransitive verb

1: to conduct oneself in an arrogant or <u>superciliously pompous</u> manner; ESPECIALLY : to walk with an air of overbearing self- confidence

transitive verb**:** to force by argument or threat**:** ***bully***

Words have power and force behind them. Whatever we speak manifests behind what we say. We have been experiencing more bullying in society than ever before due to our words expressing our self-centered idolatry. Did we stop to look up the definition? No! It just sounds good, and everybody's saying it.

Proverbs 18:21- ASV- *Death and life are in the power of the tongue; And they that love it shall eat the fruit thereof.*

Matthew 12:37 -KJV- *For by your words you will be acquitted, and by your words you will be condemned."*

Ephesians 5:6 - ISV- *Do not let anyone deceive you with meaningless words, for it is because of these things that God's wrath comes on those who are disobedient.*

2 Timothy 2:14 - KJV - *Of these things put them in remembrance, charging them before the Lord that they strive not about words to no profit, but to the subverting of the hearers.*

2 Timothy 2:15 - KJV- *Study to show thyself approved unto God, a workman that needeth not to be ashamed, rightly dividing the word of truth*

2 Timothy 2:16 - KJV- *But shun profane and vain babblings: for they will increase unto more ungodliness.*

Well, with that thought in mind, research how many children have been bullied in schools, on the streets. How many adults have been violently attacked for no reason and knocked out cold on the streets? **Words** . . . . Have we considered the vast amounts of taxpayer dollars that have gone into social programs to address bullying in schools, workplace, or the internet??? **Words** . . . . .

The word swag indicates a self-confident, cocky, boastful bully with pants hanging low between two poles (legs of our male youth who think this is fashionable status). This look is indicative of an incarcerated prisoner. His pants lowered in this manner projects a message that decrees the intentional employment of his body to another inmate.

Little folding of the hands to sleep: So shall thy poverty come as one that travelleth, and thy want as an armed man.

If there is a time warranted for the woman to know her purpose, it's now. Her children need her instructional wisdom, tender loving care, and fervent prayers.

The word intended is "**sway**" meaning: a slow movement back and forth: a controlling force or influence; the action or an instance of swaying or of being swayed : an oscillating, fluctuating, or sweeping motion; a controlling influence; the ability to exercise influence or authority : dominance

Synonyms: impact, influence, mark, repercussion, effect

Source: Merriman Webster Dictionary

Watch God move on your behalf when you begin calling things that be not as though they were with your children, family, business, and society. Being precise in your words spoken for indeed it will manifest. Here's a simple example we've all seen or heard.

Have you ever watched people with pets come out of their homes, calling them when they're no place insight? Have you ever been to a football game, and amid thousands, you call out your child's name even though you don't see them? That call is demanding; they show up because of relationship and ownership! Although they don't see you, they hear you out of all the extraneous noise, and masses of people they will automatically respond manifesting their presence to you. It's the same way with your purpose and the business inside you. To decree, and demand what belongs to you to come forth, you should have an expectancy of its arrival by speaking the right words. Selah

GEMS: "I did my best, and God did the rest. "-**Hattie McDaniel**

CHAPTER FOUR

WHAT IS THE KINGDOM OF GOD?

The Kingdom of God or the Kingdom of Heaven is a real government originated and established by God Himself. It's Capitol is Heaven, and the Body of Christ are citizens of this government. For too long, the Body of Christ has been blinded by the lack of teaching regarding God's Kingdom. The teaching had been erroneously given that when we get to heaven, there's a mansion awaiting us, but only when we get to heaven. This erroneous teaching has prevented the advancement of the Kingdom of God from manifesting. The Message of Jesus Christ is the Kingdom of God is at Hand.

Mark 1:14-15-KJV - *Now after that John was put in prison, Jesus came into Galilee, preaching the gospel of the kingdom of God, And saying, The time is fulfilled, and the kingdom of God is at hand: repent ye, and believe the gospel.*

Matthew 4:17-KJV - *From that time Jesus began to preach, and to say, Repent: for the kingdom of heaven is at hand.*

Matthew 6:33 - KJV - *But seek ye first the kingdom of God, and his righteousness; and all these things shall be added unto you.*

Genesis 1:28 is full of key study words. Notice, "God blessed them." **Blessed** means empowered, to rule, reign, in the realm given you royally. These are the aspects of the Kingdom of God that Jesus preached and taught. You have dominion, dominion rule, dominion realm, dominion reign, and dominion royalty. The Kingdom of God is superior to any form of human government. God has appointed Jesus Christ as King of the Kingdom, and He has authority over its government and subjects. Mankind cannot conceptualize the authority and power of Jesus Christ. He's seated at the Right Hand of The Father. Power and authority is given to the Body of Christ and He's interceding for us at the same time.

Matthew 28:18-KJV - *And Jesus came and spake unto them, saying, All power is given unto me in heaven and in earth.*

Matthew 4:23-KJV— *And Jesus went about all Galilee, teaching in their synagogues, and preaching the gospel of the kingdom, and healing all manner of sickness and all manner of disease among the people.*

Jesus said we would do greater things for the Kingdom of God than His cousin John the Baptist.

Luke 7: 24-29-KJV - *And when the messengers of John were departed, he began to speak unto the people concerning John, What went ye out into the wilderness for to see? A reed shaken with the wind? But what went ye out for to see? A man clothed in soft raiment? Behold, they which are gorgeously apparelled, and live delicately, are in kings' courts. But what went ye out for to see? A prophet? Yea, I say unto you, and much more than* *a prophet. This is he, of whom it is written, Behold, I send my messenger before thy face, which shall prepare thy way before thee. For I say unto you, Among those that are born of women there is not a greater prophet than John the Baptist: but he that is least in the Kingdom of God is greater than he. And all the people that heard him, and the publicans, justified God, being baptized with the baptism of John.*

Religious and traditionalists individuals reject Jesus teaching. This is the same manner today. The spirit of anti-christ is prevalent globally.

Luke 7:30-35-KJV - *But the Pharisees and lawyers rejected the counsel of God against themselves, being not baptized of him. And the Lord said, Whereunto then shall I liken the men of this generation? and to what are they like? They are like unto children sitting in the marketplace, and calling one to another, and saying, We have piped unto you, and ye have not danced; we have mourned to you, and ye have not wept. For John the Baptist came neither eating bread nor drinking wine; and ye say, He hath a devil. The Son of man is come eating and drinking; and ye say, Behold a gluttonous man, and a winebibber, a friend of publicans and sinners! But wisdom is justified of all her children. God's Kingdom is everlasting and has no date of termination.*

Daniel 2:44-KJV - *And in the days of these kings shall the God of heaven set up a kingdom, which shall never be destroyed: and the kingdom shall not be left to other people, but it shall break in pieces and consume all these kingdoms, and it shall stand for ever.*

Matthew 6:9-10-KJV - *After this manner therefore pray ye: Our Father which art in heaven, Hallowed be thy name. **Thy kingdom come. Thy will be done in earth, as it is in heaven.***

Luke 11:2-KJV - *And he said unto them, When ye pray, say, Our Father which art in heaven, Hallowed be thy name. Thy kingdom come. Thy will be done, as in heaven, so in earth.*

Acts 10: 34-35-KJV - *Then Peter opened his mouth, and said, Of a truth I perceive that God is no respecter of persons: But in every nation he that feareth (reverences) Him, and worketh righteousness, is accepted with Him.*

2 Corinthians 5:20-21-KJV - *Now then we are ambassadors for Christ, as though God did beseech you by us: we pray you in Christ's stead, be ye reconciled to God. For he hath made Him to be sin for us, who knew no sin; that we might be made the righteousness of God in Him.*

Those that receive Jesus as Lord and Savior are the ambassadors of God's Kingdom on earth. An ambassador has diplomatic immunity when executing business on behalf of his/her king, queen, or president. Being an ambassador has its perks. You may be assigned a Third World country that is barren, the people are destitute and living conditions unbearable, but you the ambassador lack for nothing while living lavishly and having all accommodations at your fingertips. You're exempt from specific laws of the land and taxes of that nation. You represent authority from the one who sent you.

An ambassador is given a title to his or her Name - Ambassador is the title. The words Extraordinary and Plenipotentiary is added when the Ambassador is acting as Head of Mission.

Look at this definition from dictionary.com - **a diplomatic official of the highest rank**, sent by one sovereign or state to another as its resident representative (Ambassador Extraordinary and Plenipotentiary). A diplomatic official of the highest rank sent by a government to represent it on a temporary mission, as for negotiating a treaty.

The same definition applies to the ambassador plenipotentiary. The Word *plenipotentiary* (from the Latin plenus "full" and potens "powerful") signifies to us the spiritual responsibilities we have from God Who sent us in the Name of His Son with an assignment to fulfill on earth. The assignment is on earth, not in heaven.

The Ambassador has to execute **a treaty that must be ratified** on earth. **A treaty is a formally concluded and ratified agreement** between countries. It's an agreement, settlement, protocol, contract, covenant, promise or pledge. We have this assignment as God's representatives in the earth. God's Word has been settled, it's contractual, it's a pledge, an authoritative covenant that denotes its protocol when applied. What an excellent and powerful assignment Ambassadors of Christ are sent with the Gospel of Jesus Christ to preach, teach the Kingdom of God. That message we're responsible for has been ratified. Pause and think about that. Selah

Now view the definition of the Ambassador at Large. To be an Ambassador at Large means you an ambassador who is not assigned to a particular diplomatic post, but you're appointed on a special mission. An **A**mbassador-at-Large is either a diplomat, a secretary or a minister **of the highest rank. He or she is accredited to represent his or her country and its people internationally.**

Matthew 28:18 - 20- KJV - *And Jesus came and spake unto them, saying, All power is given unto me in heaven and in earth. Go ye therefore, and teach all nations, baptizing them in the name of the Father, and of the Son, and of the Holy Ghost: Teaching them to observe all things whatsoever I have* commanded you: and, lo, I am with you alway, even unto the end of the world. Amen.

Mark 16:15-18 KJV- *And He said unto them, Go ye into all the world, and preach the gospel to every creature. He that believeth and is baptized shall be saved; but he that believeth not shall be damned. And these signs shall follow them that believe; In my name shall they cast out devils; they shall speak with new tongues; They shall take up serpents; and if they drink any deadly thing, it shall not hurt them; they shall lay hands on the sick, and they shall recover.*

Understanding that an Ambassador-in-Residence is usually limited to a country or embassy, the ambassador-at-large is operating in several neighboring countries, regions and can be assigned a seat in an international organization like the United Nations and the European Union.

Galatians 3:15-18-ESV - *To give a human example, brothers: even with a man-made covenant, no one annuls it or adds to it once it has been ratified. Now the promises were made to Abraham and to his offspring. It does not say, "And to offsprings," referring to many, but referring to one, "And to your offspring," who is Christ. This is what I mean: the law, which came 430 years afterward, does not annul a covenant previously ratified by God, so as to make the promise void. For if the inheritance comes by the law, it no longer comes by promise; but God gave it to Abraham by a promise.*

Why then the law? It was added because of transgressions, until the offspring should come to whom the promise had been made, and it was put in place through angels by an intermediary. Now an intermediary implies more than one, but God is one. Is the law then contrary to the promises of God? Certainly not! For if a law had been given that could give life, then righteousness would indeed be by the law. But the Scripture imprisoned everything under sin, so that the promise by faith in Jesus Christ might be given to those who believe. Now before faith came, we were held captive under the law, imprisoned until the coming faith would be revealed. So then, the law was our guardian until Christ came, in order that we might be justified by faith. But now that faith has come, we are no longer under a guardian, for in Christ Jesus you are all sons of God, through faith. For as many of you as were baptized into Christ have put on Christ. There is neither Jew nor Greek, there is neither slave nor free, there is no male and female, for you are all one in Christ Jesus. And if you are Christ's, then you are Abraham's offspring, heirs according to promise.

To ratify the covenant makes it official! Jesus ratified this treaty in Blood. With this awesome payment for our redemption back to the Father, We must be the ambassadors of industry, arts, education, sports, media education, government, military, economics, technology, and more, reaping a harvest of souls in every realm of economics.

Love is the law of the Kingdom of God, and it's love that makes God's ambassadors of His Kingdom legislate on behalf of others. Ambassadors are the ones who literally lobby for the lost and those in need. They enter the Throne Room of God, boldly petitioning on behalf of others. They do this out of genuine love for Elohim, The Trinity.

In business, your expression of love to the world is shown by offering great products and services and ultimately providing employment for those in need. You're not to become a one-woman show. You may start your business initially as a one-woman experience, but that's not God's ultimate plan for you or your business. You must invest in others.

Matthew 22: 37-40-KJV - *Jesus said unto him, Thou shalt love the Lord thy God with all thy heart, and with all thy soul, and with all thy mind. This is the first and great commandment. And the second is like unto it, Thou shalt love thy neighbour as thyself. On these two commandments hang all the law and the prophets.*

The Kingdom of God provides from Holy Spirit the wisdom, knowledge and understanding in establishing the Kingdom of God on earth while meeting needs and glorifying God.

Isaiah 48:17, 18-KJV - *Thus saith the Lord, thy Redeemer, the Holy One of Israel; I am the Lord thy God which teacheth thee to profit, which leadeth thee by the way that thou shouldest go. O that thou hadst hearkened to my commandments! then had thy peace been as a river, and thy righteousness as the waves of the sea:*

The overall objective of the Kingdom of God is accomplishing the Will of God on earth in love. The Will of God was given in the Beginning of creation along with it's dominion.

Genesis 1:28-KJV - *And God blessed them, and God said unto them, Be fruitful, and multiply, and replenish the earth, and subdue it: and have dominion over the fish of the sea, and over the fowl of the air, and over every living thing that moveth upon the earth.*

Isaiah 35:1,5, 6-KJV - *The wilderness and the solitary place shall be glad for them; and the desert shall rejoice, and blossom as the rose. Then the eyes of the blind shall be opened, and the ears of the deaf shall be unstopped. Then shall the lame man leap as an hart, and the tongue of the dumb sing: for in the wilderness shall waters break out, and streams in the desert.*

Matthew 6:10-KJV - *Thy kingdom come. Thy will be done in earth, as it is in heaven.*

Revelation 21:1-4-KJV— *And I saw a new heaven and a new earth: for the first heaven and the first earth were passed away; and there was no more sea. And I John saw the holy city, new Jerusalem, coming down from God out of heaven, prepared as a bride adorned for her husband. And I heard a great voice out of heaven saying, Behold, the tabernacle of God is with men, and he will dwell with them, and they shall be his people, and God himself shall be with them, and be their God. And God shall wipe away all tears from their eyes; and there shall be no more death, neither sorrow, nor crying, neither shall there be any more pain: for the former things are passed away. And He that sat upon the throne said, Behold, I make all things new. And he said unto me, Write: for these words are true and faithful.*

GEMS: *Faith sees the invisible, believes the unbelievable, and receives the impossible.* **Corrie Ten Boom**

GEMS: *Unless we form the habit of going to the Bible in bright moments as well as in trouble, we cannot fully respond to its consolations because we lack equilibrium between light and darkness.* **Helen Keller**

GEMS: God is in control, and therefore in EVERYTHING!

CHAPTER FIVE

THE MARKETPLACE REVISITED

The marketplace is vast and quite diverse in its complexity. Yet, it's where everything operates. Let's view it by definition and then biblically.

The marketplace is a square or place in town where markets or public sales are held. The marketplace is the interpreter of supply and demand; it's the world of trade or economic activity; the everyday world or a sphere in which intangible values compete for acceptance in the marketplace of ideas. (Summarized from Merriam-Webster's Dictionary).

What is it that we don't understand about the marketplace that causes fear of entry? One primary key has been the knowledge of its existence, its benefits, and the very fact that God is the originator of the marketplace. Women have been shunned and prohibited from entering the doors of market, ministry, and employment due to ignorance of its interworking, religion, the male ego, the geopolitical cultures, and gender discrimination predominately.

To be kept out of an existence prohibits knowledge abounding. Notice, I'm not referring to skillset. The skillset is apparent, but the forbiddance of entry halts expertise and performance. If knowledge has been the issue, let's resolve it.

The key to becoming an infamous female entrepreneur is placing God first in all we do. He is our priority and the key to our success. We need to study God's business operation plan for clarity and wisdom. We must possess the knowledge, and apply wisdom of God's Word to execute a successful business and lifestyle. Ignorance causes destruction in one's life and places you in a position of being mistreated and taken advantage of because you have no knowledge of social issues, economics, and other issues.

Hosea 4:6 KJV— My people are destroyed for lack of knowledge: because thou hast rejected knowledge, I will also reject thee, that thou shalt be no priest to me: seeing thou hast forgotten the law of thy God, I will also forget thy children.

Genesis 1:28 is full of key words. Notice, *"God blessed them."* Blessed means you have access as a believer in Christ Jesus to come boldly to the Throne Room of God and make a petition. Being a believer in Christ Jesus provides you with legal access to favor and inside information. We are to dominate in life, and the marketplace is included.

Notice God blessed *"them."* This includes male and female gender. God didn't decree the blessing on Adam alone, but on both Adam and Eve collectively, male and female. Seriously, has God ever created anything without purpose and effectiveness? He has given us examples throughout His Word to express the efficacy through discipline and preparation. God is pouring out His Spirit on ALL flesh in these last days. God is an equal opportunity anointer.

Joel 2:28 - ASV - *And it shall come to pass afterward, that I will pour out my Spirit upon all flesh; and your sons and your daughters shall prophesy, your old men shall dream dreams, your young men shall see visions: and also upon the servants and upon the handmaids in those days will I pour out my Spirit.*

Proverbs 6:6-11- KJV - *Go to the ant, thou sluggard;* **consider her ways, and be wise:** *Which having no guide, overseer, or ruler, Provideth her meat in the summer, and gathereth her food in the harvest. How long wilt thou sleep, O sluggard? when wilt thou arise out of thy sleep? Yet a little sleep, a little slumber, a little folding of the hands to sleep:*

So shall thy poverty come as one that travelleth, and thy want as an armed man.

Proverbs 6:6-11- Amplified Version
6 Go to the ant, O lazy one; Observe her ways and be wise,
7 Which, having no chief, Overseer or ruler,
8 She prepares her food in the summer
And brings in her provisions [of food for the winter] in the harvest.
9 How long will you lie down, O lazy one? When will you arise from your sleep [and learn self-discipline]?
10 "Yet a little sleep, a little slumber, A little folding of the hands to lie down and rest"—
11 So your poverty will come like
an approaching prowler who walks [slowly, but surely] And your need [will come] like an armed man [making you helpless].
Everything we need comes from God whose
Spirit resides inside a believer.

GEMS: "The kind of beauty I want most is the hard-to-get kind that comes from within - strength, courage, dignity." - **Ruby Dee**

CHAPTER SIX

GOD'S BUSINESS PLAN AND EXECUTIVE SUMMARY

Genesis 1:26; 28 - *And God said, Let us make man in our image, after our likeness: and let them have dominion over the fish of the sea, and over the fowl of the air, and over the cattle, and over all the earth, and over every creeping thing that creepeth upon the earth. So God created man in his own image, in the image of God created he him; male and female created he them. And God blessed them, and God said unto them, Be fruitful, and multiply, and replenish the earth, and subdue it: and have dominion over the fish of the sea, and over the fowl of the air, and over every living thing that moveth upon the earth.*

We must know God's Kingdom principles and His plan for us, which He gave at the Beginning of Creation. We understand that in verse 27 of Genesis Chapter One, God made us in His Own Image. God is Spirit, and so are we. He made us have a body that enables us to enter the earth's domain, and He provided us with a soul which is the seat of the mind, will, and emotions of man. So we are fully equipped by God to prosper and operate in the manner that He designed for us. The key to understanding God's purpose and Will for us is found in His Word. Just like a treasure map the more you read it the more in tuned you are to follow the path to your desired outcome - the treasure.

III John 2 KJV - *Beloved, I wish above all things that thou mayest prosper and be in health, even as thy soul prospereth.*

Without the Word being enacted by the believer, we cause the Word to slip away from us, losing momentum and power. That's a principle.

Hebrews 2:1 KJV - *Therefore we ought to give the more earnest heed to the things which we have heard, lest at any time we should let them slip.*

We should always seek the Word of God first and foremost. For it is He that causes us to profit. Without the profit manual you're without a job description, a business plan and its executive summary.

Isaiah 48:17 KJV - *Thus saith the Lord, thy Redeemer, the Holy One of Israel; I am the Lord thy God which teacheth thee to profit, which leadeth thee by the way that thou shouldest go.*

Look a what Jesus said:

Matthew 21:28-44 KJV - *But what think ye? A certain man had two sons; and he came to the first, and said, Son, go work today in my vineyard. He answered and said, I will not: but afterward he repented, and went. And he came to the second, and said likewise. And he answered and said, I go, sir: and went not. Whether of them twain did the will of his father? They say unto him, The first. Jesus saith unto them, Verily I say unto you,*

*That the publicans and the harlots go into the kingdom of God before you. For John came unto you in the way of righteousness, and ye believed him not: but **the publicans and the harlots believed him: and ye, when ye had seen it, repented not afterward, that ye might believe him.**
Selah . . . . .*

In **Genesis I:28** we see business terms and concepts used by God.

Genesis 1:28 KV - *And God blessed them, and God said unto them, Be fruitful, and multiply, and replenish the earth, and subdue it: and have dominion over the fish of the sea, and over the fowl of the air, and over every living thing that moveth upon the earth.*

We must know the Kingdom of God. Not knowing the Kingdom of God will cause you to lose it, and it will be given to a people who will produce fruit.

The Word of God causes you to rule, reign, in His realm of the earth as a citizen from Heaven in royalty. When you read the Word of God each day aloud (never silently to yourself), it transforms you.

Romans 12:2 KJV - *And be not conformed to this world: but be ye transformed by the renewing of your mind, that ye may prove what is that good, and acceptable, and perfect, Will of God.*

"The Word is creative, controlling, and prophetic. If we decree the Word of the Kingdom, everything on earth begins to adjust itself to fulfill the Word of God."

GEMS: *"In the beginning words were more for creation than communication. They were a response to something."*

Dr. Bill Winston

Words from your mouth will manifest or create itself in the earth. Whether that word is good or evil, it will manifest. Speak words in love and in line with the Word of God. We create with your words just as God did when He created the universe.

So understand The BLESSING; it makes everything possible. You want to know what the BLESSING entails. The more revelation of the Word you obtain, the more your faith increases. When faith merges with the BLESSING, it causes the Holy Spirit Himself to enable you to soar in wisdom, knowledge, and understanding beyond your wildest dreams and comprehension.

God blessed man abundantly out of adoration for him with benefits he didn't earn. Man needed the BLESSING in order to operate in grand capacity in the earth's realm. The BLESSING is the result of the Executive Summary of God's Business Plan for man. The Executive Summary's conclusion is HAVE DOMINION. To dominate is to rule, govern, control, manage and lead. So, let's look at the plan in verse twenty-eight, which is the process.

God told the man to:
Be fruitful
Multiply
Replenish
Subdue
Dominate

God wants us to **be profitable** from what He has already given to us. What's given to us is hidden in us and must be studied, researched, written, spoken from God's Word, and definitely heard to have faith for your manifested fruit. In order to obtain fruit, a fruitful seed has to be planted, the soil tilled, watered, and the plant pruned before the fruit is ready to be harvested.

So **faith** and **works** together are the manifested BLESSING working hand in hand.

When you hear the word **"multiply"** do you think about bearing children? Some would say if God was referring to bearing a multiplicity of children, Abraham could have been considered as sinning because he bore one legitimate son and one illegitimate son during his lifespan. Yet, his seed did produce and is still producing. So, fruitful simply means "to be productive, to produce something."

Your business and place of employment must find you fruitful. A lack of productivity means you've entered into a poverty mentality. Poverty is a lack of self-production. Being fruitful costs you something.

2 Samuel 24:24-KJV - *And the king (David) said unto Araunah, Nay; but I will surely buy it of thee at a price: neither will I offer burnt offerings unto the Lord my God of that which doth cost me nothing. So David bought the threshing floor and the oxen for fifty shekels of silver. And David built there an altar unto the Lord, and offered burnt offerings and peace offerings. So the Lord was intreated for the land, and the plague was stayed from Israel.*

Money shows where your heart is in its use.

NOTE: Have you noticed that in each case of Eve and Sarah, they "influenced" their husbands to go contrary to what God had said. For the husbands to follow their wives suggestions meant they chose to go against God and the head is whom God holds accountable. Remember, woman was fashioned from the man's rib that covered his heart.

Our significance is tremendous because we as women have dynamic influence, it's how we use it that will determine God's BLESSING or curse upon our lives. Influence is like the anointing - it's smeared on, rubbed into someone by Word, or actions. As an uncommon woman of faith, your influence must glorify God and never tear down His Holy house, The Kingdom of God and/or mankind.

Uncommon means you go contrary to the world's way of doing things. You don't sleep with the decision-maker to get a promotion. You don't sell yourself for a dress or pair of shoes. You're worth so much more than that. When you realize how much you're worth and the authority God has given you, you'll stop giving yourself away.

GEMS: *Father, in the Name of Jesus, I ask forgiveness of all my sins I have committed against You, your people, and especially against myself. You have made me in Your image, so I repent earnestly and turn from my sinful actions and decisions and pursue You with everything within me.*

Proverbs 14:1-KJV - *Every wise woman buildeth her house: but the foolish plucketh it down with her hands.*

Build yourself and your business literally upon the Word of God and operate in character and integrity. This makes you successful. Pursuing God causes you to be successful, not you pursuing success. To build in Hebrew is "banah" and it means to literally or figuratively build, rebuild, establish, restore, cause to continue (a house, a family). You should desire to establish your business and build a legacy that will be honored.

James 2:20-KJV - *But wilt thou know, O vain man, that faith without works is dead?*

God never tells us to do something that we aren't capable of doing. We see that dream within us, and we think it's too enormous for us to do. I don't have enough money to do that, and numerous other excuses arise to deny the calling. Money never left the earth; it's still here. Men have died and left fortunes; others have died and left opportunities and a plethora of creative ideas dormant in the land. Those ideas, gifts, abilities and talents are still here. God already provided seed for your harvest. Your gifting is hidden within you to be birthed by your faith in God's Word.

When God created Adam, He never gave him clothing or furniture. As the manager of the earth man was to create with his words what was hidden in him. Adam was clothed in the glory of God before he sinned. Being invested in the glory meant Adam's spirt was dominant and not his body.

I Corinthians 2:7-KJV - *But we speak the wisdom of God in a mystery, even the hidden wisdom, which God ordained before the world unto our glory: Which none of the princes of this world knew: for had they known it, they would not have crucified the Lord of glory.*

When Adam sinned, he knew he was naked and needed clothing; so within his view, he saw fig leaves to cover himself and his wife. Here, Adam was reacting to his flesh and not his Spirit. Notice that when one sins, it affects others. Eve, who was also clothed in the glory became naked as well. God in His mercy became the first fashion furrier and dressed them in fur, taking away the un-tailored off the rack fig leaves. This garment cost something because a blood sacrifice was made. An animal lost its life to provide his and her designer fur coats. So from the beginning, nothing created is self-made. The earth is the Lord's and the fullness thereof.

Psalms 24:1 KJV - *The earth is the Lord's, and the fulness thereof; the world, and they that dwell therein.*

Genesis 3:21-KJV - *Unto Adam also and to his wife did the Lord God make coats of skins, and clothed them.*

Management is what God gave unto man, and we must be good stewards over our personal lives. Our employment and businesses should operate in grand stewardship. By faith in God's Word, we can do anything according to the Will of God. The key is, do you believe?

Do you really believe you can jumpstart this mega-business you saw in your dreams?

James 2:19-22; 24, 26,-KJV - *Thou believest that there is one God; thou doest well: the devils also believe, and tremble. But wilt thou know, O vain man, that faith without works is dead? Was not Abraham our father justified by works, when he had offered Isaac his son upon the altar? Seest thou how faith wrought with his works, and by works was faith made perfect 24-Ye see then how that by works a man is justified, and not by faith only. 26-For as the body without the Spirit is dead, so faith without works is dead also.*

Next, God said to **"Multiply"**

Multiply means to "Reproduce what you produced." Here's a significant example: McDonald's produced the "Big Mac" and the creators of this business reproduced what they produced globally. You can go anywhere in the world and find yourself a Big Mac made the same way, same size, same taste.

Why would one decide to go globally unless they had in their hearts to dominate their area of industry? Every successful corporation on earth has become successful by following the principles of the Kingdom of God. Whether they knew it or not, they became prosperous. Wake up Church! Today, there's a crisis in the earth, and crisis attracts creativity. We have God's plan and have avoided it, rejected it, or not been taught His plan. It is Holy Spirit that causes men to be saved and man has the responsibility of discipleship teaching and equipping the Body of Christ so men and women can do the work of the ministry. It's your business to **REPLENISH, REPRODUCE WHAT'S BEEN PRODUCED!**

Ephesians 4:11-16-KJV - *And He (Jesus) gave some, apostles; and some, prophets; and some, evangelists; and some, pastors and teachers; For the perfecting of the saints, for the work of the ministry, for the edifying of the body of Christ: Till we all come in the unity of the faith, and of the knowledge of the Son of God, unto a perfect man, unto the measure of the stature of the fulness of Christ: That we henceforth be no more children, tossed to and fro, and carried about with every wind of doctrine, by the sleight of men, and cunning craftiness, whereby they lie in wait to deceive; But speaking the truth in love, may grow up into him in all things, which is the head, even Christ: From whom the whole body fitly joined together and compacted by that which every joint supplieth, according to the effectual working in the measure of every part, maketh increase of the body unto the edifying of itself in love.*

To **"edify"** means the act of building up; the act of one who promotes another's growth in Christian wisdom, piety, happiness, and holiness.

Consider, you the entrepreneur who has established a business and now has employees. It's your responsibility as the employer to train, teach, equip your employees in their job description to perform the job efficiently.

Secondarily, allocate adequate wisdom and education for them to be equipped for what God has called them to do. At their request to go forward with God's plan for their lives, speak the BLESSING of God upon them. They should have demonstrated performance in submission, character and integrity prior to their request. If those characteristics aren't present, you have more work to do in training and equipping them, and you should inform them of such.

Notice, Jesus was on earth 33 years and three of those years He selected His team and began training them. He knew their characteristics because He asked questions to locate heart motive. By doing this, He knew what each one needed and how they would respond. What's so exciting is this; Jesus knew that Judas was stealing from the treasury. He knew Judas would betray Him, yet Jesus never fired Judas or asked Him to leave. He gave Judas timeless opportunity to get it right. Based on Judas lack of character and integrity he hung himself from the rope of love extended to him by Christ Jesus.

I'm not saying to you that if you have an employee that is wayward, defiant, lacking productivity that you should maintain that person on the payroll and harm the integrity of your business. I am saying that's where quarterly reviews are applied and a one on one coaching session. When you have a defiant employee that defies your every whim, coaching now becomes counseling, which leads to dismissal. This is why you should maintain the Word of God in the workplace, beginning each day in prayer.

I gave you the example of McDonald's reproduction process, allow me to provide another Chick Fil A. Chick Fil A never opens its doors on Sunday in honoring the Sabbath Day given by God.

Isaiah 58:12-14 KJV - *And they that shall be of thee shall build the old waste places; thou shalt raise up the foundations of many generations; and thou shalt be called The repairer of the breach, The restorer of paths to dwell in.*

If thou turn away thy foot from the sabbath, from doing thy pleasure on my holy day; and call the sabbath a delight, and the holy of Jehovah honorable; and shalt honor it, not doing thine own ways, nor finding thine own pleasure, nor speaking thine own words: then shalt thou delight thyself in Jehovah; and I will make thee to ride upon the high places of the earth; and I will feed thee with the heritage of Jacob thy father: for the mouth of Jehovah hath spoken it.

Because of the faith and belief in God, Founder Truett Cathy stressed the importance of closing on Sundays to enable his employees to rest and worship if they choose — a practice that is continually practiced. There are occasions of first responder situations that Cathy's company will open on Sunday and aid mankind in the dilemma they may be experiencing.

CHAPTER SEVEN

THE MARKETPLACE NEEDS LABORERS

The uncommon woman of faith today knows she has to go the extra mile. That extra mile includes educating oneself and staying abreast of the industry changes. Being complacent and satisfied to be where you are in your knowledge level will prove detrimental to you and your business.

Going the extra mile is a virtue that has diminishing facades in society today. That extra mile has a negative drawback. The business climate and social cultures are de-sensitized. A vast majority of the market only reacts to personal needs. By going the extra mile you will experience tangible benefits. To go out of your way to help someone else in their business by bartering or recommending a product or service has a Biblical approach of sowing and reaping attributes.

In business, the acronym ROI is the Return On Investment. God will compensate your acts of love towards one another. What you sow, you will also reap. I recommend highly being a part of a business alliance that is conducive to networking with people that go the extra mile. People who take time to assist you and share business insights are genuinely for you.

Business alliances are pivotal because Christian entrepreneurs must know prayer is important and aids in business decisions, dilemmas, and issues that may arise. Prayer is the extra mile that opens doors and propels you to your destiny. Networking with invaluable people who pray is a paramount investment. You want to surround yourself with influential, knowledgeable, and anointed entrepreneurs. During this time of networking you need to glean from your circle of influence. This makes you an invested person ready to aid another. God will make sure you receive a return on your investment in people.

Refrain from becoming enamored with your name being in lights. Focus on what God has given you to do. People may not know your name nor your business initially, but God knows. Before you realize it, you're named among the exceptional.

Look at the chosen disciple Matthias in Acts 1:21- 26.

Acts 1:21 -26 - KJV - *Wherefore of these men which have companied with us all the time that the Lord Jesus went in and out among us, Beginning from the baptism of John, unto that same day that he was taken up from us, must one be ordained to be a witness with us of his resurrection. And they appointed two, Joseph called Barsabas, who was surnamed Justus, and **Matthias**. And they prayed, and said, Thou, Lord, which knowest the hearts of all men, shew whether of these two thou hast chosen, That he may take part of this ministry and apostleship, from which Judas by transgression fell, that he might go to his own place. And they gave forth their lots; and the lot fell upon **Matthias;** and he was numbered with the eleven apostles.*

Matthias is chosen by the disciples whom Jesus had chosen. They decided to fill the vacant office of Judas. They overlooked the fact the disciples were chosen by God and not by men. They ignored that fact and initiated filling the vacancy. Although overriding God's selection process Matthias had been elected. One valid point was that the disciples decided from among them because Matthias had been a follower of Jesus before his selection. Jesus made more disciples than twelve. The twelve were His staff, but He had three that were His inner court, His influencers. Jesus had men and women followers. The majority of the women followers were wealthy and provided for the ministry of Jesus Christ.

Luke 8:1-3-KJV - *After this, Jesus traveled about **from** one town and village to another, proclaiming the good news of **the** kingdom **of** God. **The** Twelve were with Him, and also some **women who** had been cured of evil spirits and diseases: Mary (called Magdalene) from whom seven demons had come out; Joanna the wife of Chuza, **the** manager of Herod's household; Susanna; and many others. These women were helping to support them out **of** their own means.*

When Jesus radically changes the life of a person, they automatically desire to fund His ministry. It is so essential to be Christ-centered, not financially centered, in your lifestyle. Love abounds from a Christ-centered individual, and giving is a joy for them.

This Scripture is explicit that women were funding His ministry at a high level. Women are statistically more generous in their giving than men. So, why are they left out of the vision when they funded the vision? This is another reason why God is calling women out of the caves. Women have been hiding in caves unjustly. Because women wear a myriad of hats, they produce a reservoir of resources. Resources translated in

Greek can mean property, possessions, resources, or means. Women bring more than bacon to the table.

Observe, Joanna, is the only follower and disciple of Christ with a husband noted here in this Scripture. Mary Magdalene and Susanna appear single. So, obviously, their money belonged solely to them. How they obtained, these financial resources was their business. They could have been entrepreneurs like Lydia and Priscilla. Others could have been widows heavily compensated. But neither of these women other than Joanna had personal resources connected to a husband. Jesus had many followers in His ministry who went on His journeys teaching and preaching the Kingdom of God and healing the sick, and a grand number were women, wealthy women.

Jesus never denied women from following Him. Jesus is not a respecter of persons, He is a respecter of faith, and these women had it. Their financial support of His ministry was their heartfelt giving in the work of the ministry.

Let's get back to Matthias, who was numbered with the eleven making it the **TWELVE**. Notice, the only time you heard his name in Scriptures was in Acts 1:23 and 26. From that point, Matthias was one of the twelve. He was a team player, doing the work of the ministry.

Acts 2:1-4 - KJV - *And when the day of Pentecost was fully come, **they were all with one accord in one place.** And suddenly there came a sound from heaven as of a rushing mighty wind, and it filled all the house where they were sitting. And there appeared unto them cloven tongues like as of fire, and it sat upon each of them. And they were all filled with the Holy Ghost, and began to speak with other tongues, as the Spirit gave them utterance*

Acts 2:14 -KJV - *But Peter, standing up with the eleven,* *lifted up his voice, and said unto them, Ye men of Judaea, and all ye that dwell at Jerusalem, be this known unto you, and hearken to my words:*

Acts 6:2-4 -KJV - *Then the twelve* *called the multitude of the disciples unto them, and said, It is not reason that we should leave the word of God, and serve tables. Wherefore, brethren, look ye out among you seven men of honest report, full of the Holy Ghost and wisdom, whom we may appoint over this business. But we will give ourselves continually to prayer, and to the ministry of the word.*

Acts 19:6-8 KJV - *And when Paul had laid his hands upon them, the Holy Ghost came on them; and they spake with tongues, and prophesied. **And all the men were about twelve.** And he went into the synagogue, and spake boldly for the space of three months, disputing and persuading the things concerning the kingdom of God.*

So, here we see evidence that we may not have our name in lights or be a household name spoken of but God knows your value, your work and your name.

Hebrews 6:10-12- KJV - *For God is not unrighteous to forget your work and labour of love, which ye have shewed toward his name, in that ye have ministered to the saints, and do minister. And we desire that every one of you do shew the same diligence to the full assurance of hope unto the end: That ye be not slothful, but followers of them who through faith and patience inherit the promises.*

People should feel a sense of confidence in being associated with a godly woman in business. An uncommon woman of faith in the marketplace will not accept mediocrity in her personal life nor in business. She is a woman of tenacity and drive. This rationale is due to her purpose in life given her by God. Before conception in the womb, the divine purpose was given. God rewards the righteous and the diligent in their business endeavors.

The desire to glorify God in business will refrain you from sharing your dreams or vision with everyone. There are times to be quiet and pursue the plan before you.

I Thessalonians 4:11-KJV- *And that ye study to be quiet, and to do your own business, and to work with your own hands, as we commanded you; That ye may walk honestly toward them that are without, and that ye may have lack of nothing.*

Matthew 7:6- ASV - *Give not that which is holy unto the dogs, neither cast your pearls before the swine, lest haply they trample them under their feet, and turn and rend you.*

Your vision or dream is holy from God. It is a profound decree from God for you to fulfill. When God gives a vision or assignment, that vision is for you only. You cannot assign it to someone else.

Romans 11:29 - KJV - *For the gifts and calling of God are without repentance.*

For a woman to become an entrepreneur means freedom and flexibility. She is not bound by a 9 to 5 workday because she can efficiently delegate tasks to others. She applies foresight to excel in business. She is free to support the ministries of God that are doing the work. She restores the breach by building communities, orphanages, providing work-related training, developing infrastructures. Her independence allows her to take a vacation whenever she deems necessary.

Isaiah 58:12 - KJV - *And they that shall be of thee shall build the old waste places: thou shalt raise up the foundations of many generations; and thou shalt be called, The repairer of the breach, The restorer of paths to dwell in.*

The development of indispensable relationships is a high commodity for the uncommon woman of faith in the marketplace. God-given relationships assist in fulfilling the call on your life and establishing camaraderie among the ranks. A woman providing individuals leadership and organizational skills enhances your business economy.

As entrepreneurs we should always provide practical means of training by which the less fortunate can attain ownership in a business or an industry for themselves.

Relationship and discipleship assists others in their calling from God preventing fear and agony.

GEMS: Don't agonize, organize. -**Florynce Kennedy**

****

CHAPTER EIGHT

THE JUGGERNAUT PROPHECY

Micah 4:13 (MSG) On your feet, Daughter of Zion! Be threshed of chaff, be refined of dross. I'm remaking you into a people invincible, into God's juggernaut to crush the godless peoples. You'll bring their plunder as holy offerings to God, their wealth to the Master of the earth.

This passage of Scripture refers to Israel obtaining victory over their enemies and bringing in the spoils and dedicating them to God. It refers to victory over its enemies. Each time Israel had gone to war God has given them land expansion. This Scripture aligns itself with Psalms 83 in dealing with today's issues and the nations vying against Israel and her land

While in Brussels, Belgium trying to sleep before my morning departure home to the United States of America. I kept seeing this one word all night long in my spirit slowly going across as if on a movie screen. The word was "juggernaut." I've heard this word but it wasn't included in my day to day jargon, so I was unsure of its meaning. I commenced to call my husband around 3 AM in the morning Belgium time and told him what had occurred. He immediately gave me the definition of juggernaut. When my husband gave the definition I cried out "Oh my precious Lord, what are You saying to me and what's next in my life that You have planned?" UNSTOPPABLE!

Definition: Juggernaut - a massive inexorable force, campaign, movement, or object that crushes whatever is in its path,(Merriman Webster).

In current English usage, juggernaut is a literal or metaphorical force described as mercilessly destructive and unstoppable. This usage originated around the 1850's.

It's normal for me to hear from God around July of each year regarding what's ahead for the next year and sometimes for the next two years. It's also unique that the Lord gives me words I don't utilize in my day to day language or even words that I emphatically have never heard of. He speaks to me regarding His plan of action that I or the church are to be involved in. After receiving the word juggernaut I began my briefing with God and my searching the Scriptures. My faith is being activated at a higher level as I begin to question how, when, where, why, what time? Most of the time I don't receive an immediate response from God; that's when I know to be very attentive to Holy Spirit and examine the Scriptures more regarding an unstoppable, destructive and merciless force.

Throughout this time-period, there's the warfare of the enemy with hindrances, blockages, or whatever or whomever he can use to try to get me distracted or disgusted. Despite the challenges, God confirms His Word to me to endure hardness and stand firmly fixed, rooted, grounded and focused on Him.

Don't get me wrong, I have allowed distractions to enter in but as we engage further into our end-time pursuit of the Kingdom of God and the marketplace we must discipline ourselves to stay on target. Pray and listen.

Within two weeks of hearing this word from God, I received a prophetic word on August 20, 2017 that I will summarize and share with you from Lana Vawser this public information. This word confirmed so much for me, allow me to bless you with it. This prophecy was directed to the Daughters of God that are rising up stronger than ever before. The Scripture God revealed to Prophetess Vawser was Micah 4:13

Micah 4:13 - ESV- *Arise and thresh, O daughter of Zion, for I will make your horn iron, and I will make your hoofs bronze; you shall beat in pieces many peoples; and shall devote their gain to the Lord, their wealth to the Lord of the whole earth.*

The Message Bible Translation is what clearly made the vision of the word juggernaut receptive to me.

Micah 4:13 MSG Bible - *"On your feet, Daughter of Zion! Be threshed of chaff, be refined of dross. I'm remaking you into a people invincible, into God's juggernaut to crush the godless peoples. You'll bring their plunder as holy offerings to God, their wealth to the Master of the earth."*

Many women have been in very intense battles but they have obtained strength from the Spirit of God that birthed strength and courage in them. Holy Spirit was strengthening them by the wind of His Spirit to get on their feet and go forward. These women have deep roots embedded into the Heart of Jesus Christ. Great work within them and as they began to arise the Lion of Judah began roaring.

Women had been in the fire, wrestling in intensity and onslaught of numerous battles but they trusted in Jesus. They have now found the Roar of God's authority in themselves and they now arise in victory. They now have their true identity and destiny for their lives. They're hearing the Voice of God and He's telling them how powerful they are in every sphere of influence He's placed in them. Suddenly all the lies and captivity of their minds, hearts and souls are falling off. There is now an accelerated deliverance taking place. The chains that had them bound are now falling off. There's healing taking place and God's positioning His daughters.

What was remarkable was that many of God's daughters didn't realize they were in battles and God is now using them in great preparation. The very place that the battle was screaming death to them and saying that they weren't going to make it is now the very birthing room of their testing which is being released. They now know who they are, their identity is being manifested. These women now have their roar restored. These women are being raised up in unity. God's daughters are being raised as **juggernauts** in Him; they're **UNSTOPPABLE IN CHRIST JESUS!** No longer will they be held back, they are being empowered and strengthened as **UNSTOPPABLE!**

(What was so amazing to me was that God was confirming His direct word to me **"JUGGERNAUT"** which is a huge, powerful, and overwhelming force (Google definition).

Women rising up like flames of fire because of God's Word giving them 20/20 vision. Women arising from slavery and bondage that held them back for so long. Rising up to a new freedom which was already theirs. The fire and roar in them is being released within them awakening them and sending them into the enemy's camp to burn his plans and schemes. They are burning the assignments against them and those in cities and nations of the world. These women are going into areas that the enemy had set up camp and God's Presence through them is causing a shifting in atmospheres, igniting breakthroughs, bringing healing and activating breakthrough in destiny points. The enemy has attempted to set up camps, attempting to cover the strategic breakthroughs and destiny points that God's daughters with eyes of fire can see/penetrate where to destroy. The enemy will try to tell them "you're going blind, you cannot see what God is doing." The truth is that the fire God has given His daughters is greater discernment and insight, greater levels of vision. It was during the battle that God was giving 20/20 vision and authority in the areas they fought.

These women are going in like flames of fire with The Word of God and activation is taking place, strategic breakthroughs and destiny points in the lives of individuals, in churches, in families, in cities, in nations. The Word will suddenly erupt like never seen before. The daughters of God will gather the spoils and will be positioned in positions of influence overnight. There will be significant demonstrations of the "gathering of the spoils" in this season. Women of God demonstrating courage and fearlessness they've never experienced are taking back what the enemy stole from them.

The favor of God will rest upon these women and they will have radical increase of God's favor in this season. There will be ripple effects of breakthrough and portals for encounter and revelation opening up to them everywhere they go. They will carry God's language and their mouths will be filled with the right words at the right time wherever they go. The hearts of God's daughters will be drawn unto Him. Destiny within their hearts will be awakened and people will experience God's Glory wherever they go. God's daughters will be used to shift the belief system in the world concerning God and Who He really is. These women will be raised up and sent out with specific revelation of God's heart and prophetic insight. The words they carry will turn many to God.

In this vision was seen the words UNDERCOVER SPECIALISTS, REVIVALISTS AND NEW ASSIGNMENTS. The Lord was seen giving many of His daughters in this season "new jackets" and on the back of these jackets were these words written. On the cuff of these jackets was the word "MARKETPLACE." The knowing came right away that God was releasing many of His daughters into the marketplace in this season that hadn't been there before. He was releasing NEW ASSIGNMENTS to those already in the marketplace. God spake these words, "There is significant increase of My Fire, My Anointing and My Favor upon My daughters already in the marketplace and others now going in. There are new assignments and great favor and influence being released upon them."

The time is come upon the Church right now where My daughters are being raised up in positions of the marketplace. There will be an increase of the revivalist anointing with signs and wonders following like that of Kathryn Kuhlman and Maria Woodworth-Etter. There will be a major healing and revival fire of God's Spirit that will be released significantly in the marketplace through God's daughters. In the marketplace many shall come to know Jesus and obtain a deep place of intimacy with Him. Many will be healed in the marketplace through a major healing wave. Daughters of God are being positioned in the marketplace to see the fire of God's Presence released and the glorious shifts that will take place."

They are moving into this increase with angelic protection and they have been well prepared for such a time as this. Whether these women know what they're doing or not it doesn't matter because God only asks for them to open their mouths and He will fill it. God never sends His people unprepared. When these women step into these overnight shifts and new assignments in the marketplace it may appear daunting, but when they step in they will be filled with joy and awe realizing what God has done with and through them.

Transformation will take place in the marketplace through women. There will also appear the rise of mothers who the enemy told they weren't important. These mothers will have greater dreams and visions that will impact training their children for future destinies. These stay at home mothers will become authors and write books and songs. Angels are landing in their homes and God is downloading things He wants them to say in book form. From Busy to Business these mothers will change their children and their communities. An entrepreneurial spirit is coming upon and new grace will rest upon them. They will perform business from home with ease and increase. They will write words of life. God has related a scribe anointing that will bring about change agents in the literary field. Supernatural writings of life, and songs, will come forth.

God's daughters in media will have Breaking News. They will be sent into the newsrooms, radio, television, movies and other media outlets in the world to bring God's power and presence of Kingdom release. God is taking back the realms of the media and causing revival to release His love and salvation message. The world is going to notice.

God says to His daughters that the day is upon us like never before and we are to remain close to Him and stay in His presence. Be careful not to be swayed by man but follow the prompting of Holy Spirit. Obedience is key. Sensitivity is key. The daughters of God are key in this end-time revival and outpouring of His Spirit. We must be in position taking our place. For this is our season, doors of opportunities, great favor and influence within our spheres of influence will increase because we were born for such a time as this!

This prophecy speaks highly of God's Kingdom in the marketplace with women. I have no doubt it refers to the church as well because there's an abundant harvest on the horizon and it has exponential acceleration like never before. God is moving in our behalf and the move is unstoppable. Therefore, it's time to come out of your cave of hiding. It's time to roar with victory.

Therefore, whatever is in your heart to do especially in business, apply yourself towards it. Whether it's writing the vision, jumpstarting or improving the business God is going to anoint you to do what you couldn't do before and it's not for you to become wealthy and hoard your treasures of wealth. No, you'll become wealthy and provide employment to others and you'll arise and shine in the marketplace. Men and women will desire the anointing on you and that's the opportunity to give them Jesus. This is the great and abundant harvest forthcoming.

As you notice in the prophecy, the things promised by God to women in diverse walks of life all relate to business. In comparison, if you have been in war and you've endured a great deal, God has seen your walk of faith and your tears in the night. But now, it's your time! No more delays, hindrances, blockages of the enemy shall prevail against you. The key is to remain close to God and keep Him first in your life.

Hebrews 6:9-12 - *But, beloved, we are persuaded better things of you, and things that accompany salvation, though we thus speak. For God is not unrighteous to forget your work and labour of love, which ye have shewed toward his name, in that ye have ministered to the saints, and do minister. And we desire that every one of you do shew the same diligence to the full assurance of hope unto the end: That ye be not slothful, but followers of them who through faith and patience inherit the promises.*

John 15:4-8 - *Abide in me, and I in you. As the branch cannot bear fruit of itself, except it abide in the vine; no more can ye, except ye abide in me. I am the vine, ye are the branches: He that abideth in me, and I in him, the same bringeth forth much fruit: for without me ye can do nothing. If a man abide not in me, he is cast forth as a branch, and is withered; and men gather them, and cast them into the fire, and they are burned. If ye abide in me, and my words abide in you, ye shall ask what ye will, and it shall be done unto you. Herein is my Father glorified, that ye bear much fruit; so shall ye be my disciples.*

GEMS: The woman power of this nation can be the power which makes us whole and heals the rotten community, now so shattered by war and poverty and racism. I have great faith in the power of women who will dedicate themselves wholeheartedly to the task of remaking our society.

Coretta Scott King

GEMS: Love makes your soul crawl out from its hiding place. **Zora Neale Hurston**

CHAPTER NINE

SHOULD I TITHE FROM MY BUSINESS?

Malachi 3:5-12- KJV - *And I will come near to you to judgment; and I will be a swift witness against the sorcerers, and against the adulterers, and against the false swearers, and against those that oppress the hireling in his wages, the widow, and the fatherless, and that turn aside the sojourner from his right, and fear not me, saith Jehovah of hosts. For I, Jehovah, change not; therefore ye, O sons of Jacob, are not consumed.*

From the days of your fathers ye have turned aside from mine ordinances, and have not kept them. Return unto me, and I will return unto you, saith Jehovah of hosts. But ye say, Wherein shall we return? Will a man rob God? yet ye rob me. But ye say, Wherein have we robbed thee? In tithes and offerings. Ye are cursed with the curse; for ye rob me, even this whole nation. Bring ye the whole tithe into the store-house, that there may be food in my house, and prove me now herewith, saith Jehovah of hosts, if I will not open you the windows of heaven, and pour you out a blessing, that there shall not be room enough to receive it. And I will rebuke the devourer for your sakes, and he shall not destroy the fruits of your ground; neither shall your vine cast its fruit before the time in the field, saith Jehovah of hosts. And all nations shall call you happy; for ye shall be a delightsome land, saith Jehovah of hosts.

Bring ye the WHOLE TITHE into the storehouse. The controversy with the tithe is whether to tithe ten percent of your income. "Should I tithe off the net or the gross? STOP! Do you see anywhere in this passage of Scripture where it refers to gross or net? What's relevant is God saying I WILL REBUKE THE DEVOURER FOR YOUR SAKES, The tithe brings protection and increase to you.

Psalms 24:1 - KJV - *The earth is the Lord's, and the fulness thereof; the world, and they that dwell therein.*

I Corinthians 10:26-KJV - *For the earth is the Lord's, and the fulness thereof.*

If the earth is the Lord's that means He owns 100 percent of it including you and I. So, if the tithe is the tenth and there's 90 percent left how much belongs to God? Answer - ALL 100 percent. God allows us to take the 90 percent and manage it. The tithe is for Kingdom economy not entirely for the pastor but for the work of the ministry. The pastor and his/her staff should be compensated according to the Word of God. The engagement of winning souls throughout the world requires money to travel to the nations. It takes money to go ye into all the world and plant churches.

I Timothy 5:17-18 -KJV - *Let the elders that rule well be counted worthy of double honour, especially they who labour in the word and doctrine. For the scripture saith, Thou shalt not muzzle the ox that treadeth out the corn. And, The labourer is worthy of his reward.*

So, the tithe isn't to be viewed as dollars and cents only. We are to tithe our time to God. There are twenty-four hours in a day and we should tithe a minimum of two hours and forty minutes to God personally and daily.

Bring ye ALL - what's left after ALL? Bring ye all the tenth of your resources. Think about it was Abram employed by anybody, yet he gave unto God. By not tithing from the business God has given: you assist in the lack existing in the House of God.

There are too many business people in the church today confused about whether they should tithe. Just tithe so the church won't be struggling to fulfill its mandate. It has been stated by some that only three percent of the church today actually tithe. Can you imagine the souls that can be won, homes built for the homeless, widows and orphans. Can you conceive the church providing finances into medical research for the cure of diseases? Have you ever thought about the fact that the money withheld from not tithing from your business could have saved someone from dying prematurely because your monies could have aided in their cure?

Imagine this - A church full of entrepreneurs and because they can't find literally verbatim in the Bible whether they should tithe or not - so they don't! What happens to that church? Doesn't take an Einstein to figure that out. Selah

Proverbs 3:1-10 - KJV - *My son, forget not my law; but let thine heart keep my commandments: For length of days, and long life, and peace, shall they add to thee. Let not mercy and truth forsake thee: bind them about thy neck; write them upon the table of thine heart: So shalt thou find favour and good understanding in the sight of God and man.*

Trust in the Lord with all thine heart; and lean not unto thine own understanding. In all thy ways acknowledge him, and he shall direct thy paths. Be not wise in thine own eyes: fear the Lord, and depart from evil. It shall be health to thy navel, and marrow to thy bones. Honour the Lord with thy substance, and with the firstfruits of all thine increase: So shall thy barns be filled with plenty, and thy presses shall burst out with new wine.

Be not wise in your own eyes trying to figure out a solution to avoid giving the tithe unto God. In verse nine there are key words to assist us in tithing. You can receive it or deny it; that's your prerogative. Let's view these key words from the Hebrew language:

Subtance - Hown - (Hebrew) - wealth, riches, price, high value, sufficiency

Firstfruits - Reshiyth - (Hebrew) - the first in place, time, order, or rank; chief(est), principal thing, choice part. **From the root word Rosh** - meaning sum.

Increase - tbuwah - (Hebrew) - income, produce, (lit. or fig.) fruit, gain, revenue, product, yield, crops of the earth, gain, gain of wisdom, product of lips.

Honor - kabad - (Hebrew) - to be heavy, numerous, rich, cause to make weighty, glorify, make glorious, (very) great, cause to be honored, make oneself numerous.

To have substance, and tithe from your first fruits of your increase you honor God and make him and yourself glorified.

Interesting, you should tithe from the gain of wisdom (education) to give what you've obtained in order to build or rebuild a society, an economy, a nation, a kingdom. Your business profession as a consultant, coach, minister, instructor or actor requires the use of your mouth primarily. You obtain increase financially from the words of your mouth and intellectual realm. You're profitable! Sow to yourself. Give and it shall be given unto you, good measure, pressed down, shaken together and running over shall men give unto YOU! So now, you're in a grand position to sow back into the Kingdom of God by first tithing and then giving; both go hand in hand.

From a business standpoint, how are you handling your revenue generation? As an entrepreneur always apply the 1333 Method. From your business increase tithe ten percent; this represents the 1 and it should be first. Next, pay yourself thirty percent of your income which represents 3. Following should be thirty percent for business expenses, another 3 and thirty percent for business revenues, the last 3. So, 1333 represents ten percent tithe, thirty percent salary, thirty percent expenses, and thirty percent revenue which equals 100 percent receivables.

You may decide to appropriate your revenue differently and that's your option, but this is a typical formula for a business entrepreneur.

Let's look further into Biblical accounts of wealth and the tithe.

Genesis 14:18-20-KJV - *And Melchizedek king of Salem brought forth bread and wine: and he was priest of God Most High. And he blessed him, and said, Blessed be Abram of God Most High, possessor of heaven and earth: and blessed be God Most High, who hath delivered thine enemies into thy hand. And he gave him a tenth of all.*

Where did Abram receive his wealth to tithe? Was he employed by someone so he could give of the gross or the net?

Genesis 12:10 -13:6 - KJV - *And there was a famine in the land: and Abram went down into Egypt to sojourn there; for the famine was grievous in the land. And it came to pass, when he was come near to enter into Egypt, that he said unto Sarai his wife, Behold now, I know that thou art a fair woman to look upon: Therefore it shall come to pass, when the Egyptians shall see thee, that they shall say, This is his wife: and they will kill me, but they will save thee alive. Say, I pray thee, thou art my sister: that it may be well with me for thy sake; and my soul shall live because of thee.*

And it came to pass, that, when Abram was come into Egypt, the Egyptians beheld the woman that she was very fair. The princes also of Pharaoh saw her, and commended her before Pharaoh: and the woman was taken into Pharaoh's house. And he entreated Abram well for her sake: and he had sheep, and oxen, and he asses, and menservants, and maidservants, and she asses, and camels. And the Lord plagued Pharaoh and his house with great plagues because of Sarai Abram's wife. And Pharaoh called Abram, and said, What is this that thou hast done unto me? why didst thou not tell me that she was thy wife? Why saidst thou, She is my sister? so I might have taken her to me to wife: now therefore behold thy wife, take her, and go thy way. And Pharaoh commanded his men concerning him: and they sent him away, and his wife, and all that he had.

And Abram went up out of Egypt, he, and his wife, and all that he had, and Lot with him, into the south. And Abram was very rich in cattle, in silver, and in gold. And he went on his journeys from the south even to Bethel, unto the place where his tent had been at the beginning, between Bethel and Hai; Unto the place of the altar, which he had made there at the first: and there Abram called on the name of the Lord.

And Lot also, which went with Abram, had flocks, and herds, and tents. And the land was not able to bear them, that they might dwell together: for their substance was great, so that they could not dwell together.

Notice, there was a famine. That's why Abram left to sojourn where he could find substance. Observe the Hand of God upon him and favor arises from the king and blessed him mightily. Abram was so rich that even Lot prospered because he was with him.

Genesis 13:7-11- KJV - *And there was a strife between the herdmen of Abram's cattle and the herdmen of Lot's cattle: and the Canaanite and the Perizzite dwelled then in the land. And Abram said unto Lot, Let there be no strife, I pray thee, between me and thee, and between my herdmen and thy herdmen; for we be brethren. Is not the whole land before thee? separate thyself, I pray thee, from me: if thou wilt take the left hand, then I will go to the right; or if thou depart to the right hand, then I will go to the left. And Lot lifted up his eyes, and beheld all the plain of Jordan, that it was well watered every where, before the Lord destroyed Sodom and Gomorrah, even as the garden of the Lord, like the land of Egypt, as thou comest unto Zoar. Then Lot chose him all the plain of Jordan; and Lot journeyed east: and they separated themselves the one from the other.*

Notice, it didn't matter to Abram what direction or parcel of land Lot chose because he was wealthy beyond recognition from the Blessing of God. Abram was so wealthy he had laborers working for him that he later used as an army in battle. But I still ask you was Abram working as an employee or was he the entrepreneur with employees?

Let's stop making things so difficult. At the end of the day it all boils down to a heart decision - "Do I love money more than God?"

History of the Tithe From Easton's Bible Dictionary:

Tithe, a tenth of the produce of the earth consecrated and set apart for special purposes. The dedication of a tenth to God was recognized as a duty before the time of Moses. Abraham paid tithes to Melchizedek (**Genesis 14:20; Hebrews 7:6**; and Jacob vowed unto the Lord and said, *"Of all that thou shalt give me I will surely give the tenth unto thee."*

The first Mosaic law on this subject is recorded in **Leviticus 27:30 -32.** Subsequent legislation regulated the destination of the tithes (**Numbers 18:21 -24, 26-28; Deuteronomy 12:5 6, 11, 17; Deuteronomy 12:5, 23**). The paying of the tithes was an important part of the Jewish religious worship. In the days of Hezekiah one of the first results of the reformation of religion was the eagerness with which the people brought in their tithes (**2 Chronicles 31:5 6)**. The neglect of this duty was sternly rebuked by the prophets (**Amos 4:4 Malachi 3:8 10).** The emphasis here is that it was constituted before the Law, carried on through the Law and into the New Testament. Nevertheless, the principle of this law remains, and is incorporated in the Gospel (**1 Corinthians 9:13, 14)**; and if, as is the case, the motive that ought to prompt to liberality in the cause of religion and of the service of God be greater now than in Old Testament times, then **Christians ought to go beyond the ancient Hebrew in consecrating both themselves and their substance to God.**

Every Jew was required by the Levitical law to pay three tithes of his property (1) one tithe for the Levites; (2) one for the use of the temple and the great feasts; and (3) one for the poor of the land.

Three tithes and the average church doesn't want to tithe one?

GEMS: "I have found that among its other benefits, giving liberates the soul of the giver." - **Maya Angelou**

CHAPTER TEN

FAITH IN THE MARKETPLACE

There has been an acceleration in the marketplace giving momentum to the Body of Christ. In the year 2020 we will experience the awesomeness of God's favor in operation by providing the ability of seeing, knowing and obtaining our God given heritage. Let's look at the word heritage to garner a clear perspective. Heritage defined from the Merriam Webster Dictionary states property that descends to an heir or something transmitted by or acquired from a predecessor, a legacy, or inheritance.

This prophetic word places us in good standing to repossess what was stolen, damaged, left behind, destroyed or something you're not knowledgeable of. A season of natural inheritances will become prevalent. Our heritage has dual receptivity; one of spiritual inheritance provided by Jesus Himself and of natural means provided by someone given you. Jesus provided redemption, salvation and our being seated positionally with Him in heavenly places. We also inherited authority in His Name and so much more. In this season of seeing, knowing and obtaining we shouldn't have any anxieties concerning the validity of either. God promises to perform His Word.

Matthew 6:27-33 - ESV - *And which of you by being anxious can add a single hour to his span of life? And why are you anxious about clothing? Consider the lilies of the field, how they grow: they neither toil nor spin, yet I tell you, even Solomon in all his glory was not arrayed like one of these. But if God so clothes the grass of the field, which today is alive and tomorrow is thrown into the oven, will he not much more clothe you, O you of little faith? Therefore do not be anxious, saying, 'What shall we eat?' or 'What shall we drink?' or 'What shall we wear?' For the Gentiles seek after all these things, and your heavenly Father knows that you need them all. But seek first the kingdom of God and his righteousness, and all these things will be added to you.*

Jeremiah 1:12- KJV - *Then said the Lord unto me, Thou hast well seen: for I will hasten my Word to perform it.*

Ezekiel 12:23c- 28 - ESV- *The days are near, and the fulfillment of every vision. For there shall be no more any false vision or flattering divination within the house of Israel. For I am the Lord; I will speak the Word that I will speak, and it will be performed. It will no longer be delayed, but in your days, O rebellious house, I will speak the word and perform it, declares the Lord God."*

*And the word of the Lord came to me: "Son of man, behold, they of the house of Israel say, The vision that he sees is for many days from now, and he prophesies of times far off.' Therefore say to them, Thus says the Lord God: None of my words will be delayed any longer, but **the word that I speak will be performed, declares the Lord God**."*

None of God's Words will be delayed or void of power. In the days of Ezekiel he saw the false prophets and the people of Israel in doubt of God's Word manifesting in the chapter. God's Word manifests whether in judgment or blessing. The Israelites were scattered and doubted God, yet God was their sanctuary of safety without their knowing it. In these end-times you will know God's peace and His leading by Holy Spirit Himself. He will direct you to your inheritance and to your marketable means of success as an entrepreneur. No doubting on your behalf helps the knowing bring about the seeing and straightway obtaining the promises.

Micah 2:1-2 - ESV - *Woe to them that devise iniquity, and work evil upon their beds! when the morning is light, they practice it, because it is in the power of their hand. And they covet fields, and take them by violence; and houses, and take them away: so they oppress a man and his house, even a man and his heritage.*

You may have previously encountered setbacks and delays; the wrong personnel staff or even the wrong business partner, however, that was in your past. You may have invested your personal monies to start your business and because you lacked money management skills your home and car was repossessed in the start-up phase. Trust Holy Spirit to lead and teach you. No more fear, no more stressful anxieties. If you by faith receive God's Word and by faith study and meditate upon it victory is yours The past is the past. If God wanted you to continue to look back to your past He would have placed eyes in the back of your head. You're created to go forward!

God declares no more delays. We are to receive His Word by faith. Expect to see the favor of God upon you causing real estate properties, lands, to come into your possession. This will enable you to build the old waste places and create jobs in the marketplace for others in need of employment. The heritage awaiting you will be secured by faith in God's Word. As God promised it to Moses and to Joshua, He also promised to you.

Never run from adversity or relocate without obtaining God's confirmation. Being out of position in the marketplace or in ministry can be devastating. Just as location, location is key in real estate so is it key in the Kingdom of God. God is not a respecter of persons; He's a respecter of faith.

Ezekiel 11:17-21 -ESV - *Therefore say, 'Thus says the Lord God: I will gather you from the peoples and assemble you out of the countries where you have been scattered, and I will give you the land of Israel.' And when they come there, they will remove from it all its detestable things and all its abominations. And I will give them one heart, and a new spirit I will put within them. I will remove the heart of stone from their flesh and give them a heart of flesh, that they may walk in my statutes and keep my rules and obey them. And they shall be my people, and I will be their God. But as for those whose heart goes after their detestable things and their abominations, I will bring their deeds upon their own heads, declares the Lord God."*

Joshua 1:5-9 - KJV- *There shall not any man be able to stand before thee all the days of thy life: as I was with Moses, so I will be with thee: I will not fail thee, nor forsake thee. Be strong and of a good courage: for unto this people shalt thou divide for an inheritance the land, which I sware unto their fathers to give them. Only be thou strong and very courageous, that thou mayest observe to do according to all the law, which Moses my servant commanded thee: turn not from it to the right hand or to the left, that thou mayest prosper whithersoever thou goest. This book of the law shall not depart out of thy mouth; but thou shalt meditate therein day and night, that thou mayest observe to do according to all that is written therein: for then thou shalt make thy way prosperous, and then thou shalt have good success. Have not I commanded thee? Be strong and of a good courage; be not afraid, neither be thou dismayed: for the Lord thy God is with thee whithersoever thou goest.*

I John 3:2 - KJV - *Beloved, now are we the sons of God, and it doth not yet appear what we shall be: but we know that, when* *he shall appear, we shall be like him; for we shall see him as he is.*

Hebrews 11:1-3 -KJV - *Now faith is the substance of things hoped for, the evidence of things not seen. For by it the elders obtained a good report. Through faith we understand that the worlds were framed by the word of God, so that things which are seen were not made of things which do appear.*

So many people await your call to the marketplace. Third world countries where women are abused and treated as dogs. Actually, the dogs have a better life. Girls are forbidden to enter schools for educational advancement. Widows are abandoned and left isolated and looked down upon. Your entrepreneurial calling is not for you to hoard up money and become so enamored in your wealth that you avoid the House of God. No! Your calling in the marketplace is to provide finances to the Kingdom of God enabling the Word to go forth to a lost and dying world. Your job is to remain under anointed teaching that you may obtain your assignment from God with wisdom, knowledge and understanding.

Isaiah 1:17-19 - KJV - *Learn to do well; seek judgment, relieve the oppressed, judge the fatherless, plead for the widow. Come now, and let us reason together, saith the Lord: though your sins be as scarlet, they shall be as white as snow; though they be red like crimson, they shall be as wool. If ye be willing and obedient, ye shall eat the good of the land.*

In order to start your business you **don't** have to be ready, just obedient. If God has called you to entrepreneurship just become willing and obedient.

GEMS: *Learn to be quiet enough to hear the genuine within yourself so that you can hear it in others. - **Marian Wright Edelman***

CHAPTER ELEVEN

WE CAN'T BE IDLE IN THE MARKETPLACE

Matthew 20:1-16-KJV

For the kingdom of heaven is like unto a man that is an householder, which went out early in the morning to hire labourers into his vineyard. And when he had agreed with the labourers for a penny a day, he sent them into his vineyard. And he went out about the third hour, and saw others standing idle in the marketplace, And said unto them; Go ye also into the vineyard, and whatsoever is right I will give you. And they went their way. Again he went out about the sixth and ninth hour, and did likewise. And about the eleventh hour he went out, and found others standing idle, and saith unto them, Why stand ye here all the day idle? They say unto him, Because no man hath hired us. He saith unto them, Go ye also into the vineyard; and whatsoever is right, that shall ye receive. So when even was come, the lord of the vineyard saith unto his steward, Call the labourers, and give them their hire, beginning from the last unto the first. And when they came that were hired about the eleventh hour, they received every man a penny. But when the first came, they supposed that they should have received more; and they likewise received every man a penny. And when they had received it, they murmured against the goodman of the house, Saying, These last have wrought but one hour, and thou hast made them equal unto us, which have borne the burden and heat of the day. But he answered one of them, and said, Friend, I do thee no wrong: didst not thou agree with me for a penny? Take that thine is, and go thy way: I will give unto this last, even as unto thee. Is it not lawful for me to do what I will with mine own? Is thine eye evil, because I am good? So the last shall be first, and the first last: for many be called, but few chosen.

In verse one the labourers were hired and paid a days wages equaling a denarius. This was a Roman silver coin in New Testament times which purchased about ten donkeys, which was the mode of transportation in Biblical times. A denarius contains ten. After 217 B.C. the denarius increased to 16 and became the principal coin of the Roman Empire. The denarius was now worth 16 to the laborers of the vineyard.

The householder had agreed with the labourers for a penny— a usual day's hire. He sent them into his vineyard. And he returned around the third hour being nine o'clock.

The laborers were hired at 6am, early with expectation for employment. They positioned themselves in the marketplace where business was the acumen of the times. Jesus found people "idle" in the marketplace.

The Greek word for **Idle is** "argos" meaning inactive, unemployed, lazy, useless, barren, slow; free from labor, at leisure, shunning the labor which one ought to perform.

The householder found people **"idle" in the marketplace.** Not only would there be people seeking employment in the marketplace there would be the lazy, slouthful individuals looking for a handout. These were those without an occupation, without a business, without employment, without an enterprise or undertaking. Simply put, they were without vision. **To be without vision you lack provision.**

In verse six the householder came at the eleventh hour and found more standing **"idle."** The householder spake to them inquiring "Why do you stand here **"idle."**

He saw others standing idle in the market place— **unemployed.** He saw and He acted by employing them. You can't employ someone without having a business to offer wages for their skill or labor. It's great to have employment but you'll never ever become a millionaire nor billionaire working 9am to 5pm, five to seven days a week. Yes, some people are working seven days a week. Women, foolish women of little faith are working seven days blinded by the snare satan has arranged for them. Obviously there's no time for the Word of God when working excessive hours and days. There's no time for family, no time for children, which results in no peace and early death.

A common woman who doesn't worship or fellowship with God definitely doesn't trust God for a better means of employment or a creative idea to start her own business. Without Jesus, you become a slave to the world's system and in total bondage and agreement with the enemy's plan not God's. You're content being in the cave.

Notice, about the eleventh hour, one hour before the close of the working day; a most unusual hour he found others standing idle, and saith, Why stand ye here all the day idle?—Of course they had not been there, but as they were now willing, and the day was not over, they also are engaged in employment with the same terms as the others. The point I want you to see is all day long there were people idle in the marketplace. Why? Like today, these people were abandoned, scattered abroad, neglected, wearied, fatigued, disorganized, their souls uncared for. In verse 36 the word "fainted" meant they were harassed resulting in the aforementioned.

We are His labourers, divinely qualified and called to gather in the harvest of souls in your respective areas of industry and jurisdiction. We're called to create jobs, train others to become entrepreneurs and to take care of the poor, orphaned and the widows.

For the kingdom of heaven is like unto a man that is an householder, and the depiction of a vineyard, represents the harvest of souls for heaven.

Matthew 9:37-38 - KJV - *Then saith He unto His disciples, The harvest truly is plenteous, but the labourers are few; Pray ye therefore the Lord of the harvest, that he will send (thrust) forth labourers into his harvest.*

Matthew 9:35 -KJV - *And Jesus went about all the cities and villages, teaching in their synagogues, and preaching the gospel of the kingdom, and healing every sickness and every disease among the people.*

GEMS: *We must not, in trying to think about how we can make a big difference, ignore the small daily differences we can make which, over time, add up to big differences that we often cannot foresee. -* **Marian Wright Edelman**

CHAPTER TWELVE

SUCCESS IN THE MARKETPLACE

Successful People Pray and Meditate

Joshua 1:8 - ESV - *This Book of the Law shall not depart from your mouth, but you shall meditate on it day and night, so that you may be careful to do according to all that is written in it. For then you will make your way prosperous, and then you will have good success.*

(This secret of your success is hidden in your daily routine). People are rewarded in public for what they do in private.

Invest in yourself first and then invest in others.

Romans 14:19-ESV - *So then let us pursue what makes for peace and for mutual upbuilding.*

Pray and meditate - You need a journal and a pen. Why? To record your creative ideas that provide a solution to your breakthrough. You plan your future and you should write it down. Always take a journal and a pen in your quiet time before the Lord and learn to hear His Voice

Successful people read. The more you read the more you want to read and be successful. The more you learn the more you earn. Things begin to grow. You never stop learning because you're out of school; that causes mediocrity.

Successful people listen to audio teaching. Faith comes by hearing and hearing by the Word of God.

You must renew your mind.

Write your dreams and goals – Read Napolean Hill's book - "Think and Grow Rich". **THINK IT AND INK IT**!

Successful people exercise - Invest in your body and keep your temple fit, clean and holy. Successful people rise early in meditation, prayer and reading the Word of God. Thereafter, they begin their day with marketplace strategies from heaven because their minds are fresh and alert.

Successful people listen to worship and classical music.

In order to become successful we should never engage in pursuing money. Money should be attracted to us because we have the skillset to manage it. To become successful you must apply strategy. Starting a business requires start-up capital and most importantly timing. To lack in either of these components isn't wise. Of course your start-up capital is relative based on the type of business ventured. But to open a retail clothing store very sparsely upon launch shows your lack of finances to have an adequate line of clothing in your store. This hurts your business image and potential customers see it.

Never attempt a business start-up without a plan of action and the right timing. To avoid a plan of action can cause a negative voice in the marketplace regarding you and your business. Success is thinking and performing as a citizen of the Kingdom of God.

Luke 14:28 ESV - *For which of you, desiring to build a tower, does not first sit down and count the cost, whether he has enough to complete it?*

Galatians 6:9 ESV - *And let us not grow weary of doing good, for in due season we will reap, if we do not give up.*

I Timothy 6:9-10 - ESV - *But those who desire to be rich fall into temptation, into a snare, into many senseless and harmful desires that plunge people into ruin and destruction. For the love of money is a root of all kinds of evils. It is through this craving that some have wandered away from the faith and pierced themselves with many pangs.*

GEMS: Greatness is not measured by what a man or woman accomplishes, but by the opposition he or she has overcome to reach his goals. **-Dorothy Height**

CHAPTER THIRTEEN

INVESTMENT IN THE MARKETPLACE

Luke 19:13-KJV - *And he called his ten servants, and delivered them ten pounds, and said unto them, Occupy till I come.*

The word **occupy** is pragmatism in Greek. It means to busy oneself with trade; to carry out business and to carry on the business of a banker or a trader. Both banker and trader are individuals that will obtain interest or a profit. Its root word "pragma" specifically deals with a business or commercial transaction. To dig deeper the root word of pragma is "prasso" which means to practice and/or perform repeatedly, habitually. To manage public affairs, transact public business regarding revenue, debt or tribute.

The meaning of the word **occupy** sheds more light on why Jesus told Zacchaeus "Today, is My day to be a guest in your house." Zacchaeus was a rich man, the head taxman and of the family of Abraham. In verse nine and ten of Luke 19 Jesus tells Zacchaeus today salvation comes to your house. For Zacchaeus this was a wonderful encounter to have Jesus in his home and for he and his family to receive salvation. Notice that he confesses to Jesus his faults in verse eight regarding him cheating and that he repays on his sins. He is also a giver to the poor. As a tax collector he must operate with the proper and honest means of exchange. This had to be implemented in Zaccaheus life. Jesus then begins to teach him and His disciple about investment and refraining from idleness in verses 11 through 27.

Jesus commanded them and the Body of Christ today to occupy until He comes and truly He's coming. Build the Kingdom of God on earth and profit from His Word.

Deuteronomy 8:16 KJV – *But thou shalt remember the Lord thy God: for it is He that giveth thee the power to get wealth that he may establish His covenant which He aware unto thy fathers, as it is this day.*

Isaiah 48:17 – KJV – *Thus saith the Lord, th Redeemer. The Holy One of Israel; I am The Lord thy God which teacheth thee to profit, which leadeth thee by the way that thou shouldest go.*

In the accounts of the Biblical marketplace you find the Scribes and Pharisees in the prideful pretentious manner strutting the streets of business where they could be seen. They desired recognition and fame, a desire to be worshipped. Jesus warned His disciples concerning the religious types who were full of themselves.

Matthew 23: 3-7 KJV – *"All therefore whatsoever they bid you observe, that observe and do; but do not ye after their works: for they say, and do not. For they bind heavy burdens and grievous to be borne, and lay them on men's shoulders; but they themselves will not move them with one of their fingers. But all their works they do for to be seen of men: they make broad their* *phylacteries, and enlarge the borders of their garments, And love the uppermost rooms at feasts, and the chief seats in the synagogues, And greetings in the markets, and to be called of men, Rabbi, Rabbi."*

Jesus informed His disciples that the Scribes and Pharisees were competent teachers of the law and they were astute in their teachings on Moses. But He warned them not to follow them because they were pretentious and their hearts weren't of God's love. They would issue out laws to abide by yet not one law was attributable to how one goes about living out a life that glorifies God.

They took great pleasure in watching people miss it so they could point the finger. Daily they paraded in their embroidered prayer shawls and designer robes for all to see and admire seeking flattery, and prestigious places of honor. Sounds like our marketplace today.

The highly successful worldly female executives flaunt their high scaled lifestyle of greed and glamour, sex and fashion forsaking any desire to finance advancement to remove urban blight, develop housing, create jobs or build the economic status of the urban and rural areas of society.

This is definitely why being idle in the marketplace is futile to building the Kingdom of God. God needs His people on the front lines in every sphere of society such as the arts, education, sports, entertainment, business, government and more.

When a child of God enters the entrepreneurial realm peace, joy, righteousness, love is being established because of their lifestyle. Christianity is a lifestyle. Notice, I didn't say religion is a lifestyle. Religion is what the Scribes and Pharisees were about.

The modern day religious person parties with the world, drinks with the world, operates in and loves sexual relationships. They have abortions because a child doesn't fit their lifestyle and so much more.

A wise uncommon woman of God in business lives a lifestyle of Christ Jesus and creativity is blossoming within her on a daily basis. Christianity is her lifestyle so she doesn't have to bang someone against the head to make them understand salvation and accept Jesus as their Lord. People want love inside and outside of the marketplace.

GEMS: *Just remember the world is not a playground but a schoolroom. Life is not a holiday but an education. One eternal lesson for us all: to teach us how better we should love.* -**Barbara Jordan**

CHAPTER FOURTEEN

THE GLOBAL MARKETPLACE

II Timothy 4:3-5-KJV *For the time will come when they will not endure sound doctrine; but after their own lusts shall they heap to themselves teachers, having itching ears; And they shall turn away their ears from the truth, and shall be turned unto fables. But watch thou in all things, endure afflictions, do the work of an evangelist, make full proof of thy ministry.*

In order to remain competitive in today's marketplace you must operate with a global mindset. We're in a multicultural society and the global marketplace generates an acceleration of growth with a myriad of opportunities. Attending various international conferences, summits, and symposiums can inform you of accessing a new or more advanced consumer base. This is where you'll generate new revenue for your company as well as obtaining an educational view of the companies you're involved in. To obtain an international global base gives you a highly competitive edge.

The recent rise and acceleration of information technology and communications across the globe have made diversified economies merge onto the world scene. There were economies which were isolated from each other. The current situation in the global market will help individual markets frame their own policy measures.

Global market means international interfacing of the economy by global transactions of goods and services. Pricing is determined by international demand and supply of commodities.

The global marketplace is the sum of all people from diversified cultures who desire to obtain your products and/or your services. Begin to look into import and export and its economic advantages.

To engage the global marketplace, try focusing on investments into your local markets with a global strategy that helps you obtain consistency with your brand and not lose brand identity in the global marketplace. This is termed globalization.

Globalization also implies the merge of the technology, economic, political, social and cultural spheres of the nations around the world.

Begin studying brands that are and have been in the global market for extended periods of time and haven't lost their brand identity. There's Coca-Cola, Kentucky Fried Chicken, McDonald's, Starbucks, Nike and more. Become innovative with your global entrance strategy.

Study emerging markets such as Nigeria, Democratic Republic of Congo. Africa is beginning to surge into the global marketplace with its oil and natural resources, coffee, gold, diamonds, uranium, platinum, iron ore and more.

God has you situated for such a time as this to impact the global market and its people with His economic plan. It's all about the people.

GEMS: What God intended for you goes far beyond anything you can imagine. **- Oprah Winfrey**

CHAPTER FIFTEEN

THE UNCOMMON BUSINESS WOMAN PRAYER OF FAITH

Father God, in the Name of Your Son Jesus I thank You for Your Son being born of a woman, dying on Calvary for me, descending into hell and taking authority over death, hell and the grave, ascending into Heaven and Returning again for His Church. I thank You for my salvation and for your goodness, favor and blessing upon me.

I will walk worthy of the vocation wherewith I have been called and I will be an exemplary ambassador in the marketplace for You. I thank You Holy Spirit for leading, guiding me into all truth and when I call You show me great and mighty things that I have not known and all things hidden are revealed to me. You enable me to write the vision and make it plain so that I can run with it and fulfill my goals and engagement. Because You love me You will change laws, remove one and set up another causing me to advance and remain affixed and affirmed in the marketplace and fulfilling Your plans on earth through my assignment.

I thank You that favor surrounds me as shield and causes my enemies to be at peace with me. When opportunities arise, You give me the ability to evaluate them with a clear mind and open heart. I purpose to walk in love towards all men and to give to the poor and needy. I thank You that my marketing plan aligns with the Kingdom of God and I walk in the authority of Jesus Christ. I thank You for the exponential manifestation of the blessing upon me that will cause contracts, capital, real estate, resources, personnel, sales and services to glorify You. I operate my business as unto You. I will honor Your Sabbath and be a diligent tither into the Kingdom of God and a giver to the poor. I purpose to go into all the world with my entrepreneurial expertise that You have given me making disciples, healing the sick and proclaiming the Kingdom of God on earth.

May I learn from every task presented and experience provided. I hear the Voice of God and I know what to do and what is best for my businesses. Your Blessing makes me rich and adds no toiling with it. I walk worthy of the vocation wherewith I am called and no weapon formed against me shall prosper. You teach me to profit, to tithe and to give in joy. I expect the 100 fold on my giving.

I will remember to take time for myself and for those I love. Give me the peace of mind to know that the work I perform will provide financial security for my family, and the Gospel's sake as well as my own.

Thank You Father for making me Your uncommon, extraordinary and influential businesswoman. IN JESUS NAME

Amen

04160828-0095588

Printed in the United States
By Bookmasters